aristotle®

GMAT®
Sentence Correction
GRAIL

Aristotle Prep SC Grail, 3rd Edition

10-digit International Standard Book Number: 9350872846

13-digit International Standard Book Number: 978-9350872840

Publisher: Aristotle Prep

Copyright © 2012 Aristotle Prep

Contents

Section 3 – Miscellaneous Concepts

Section 4 – Practice Set

Section 5 – The Quick Recall Section

Introduction

Sentence Correction is a topic quite dreaded by candidates taking the GMAT. Though the sheer number of concepts and rules may seem intimidating at first, with discipline and the right approach, it is not difficult to master these concepts and their application to questions. Through this book, we will take you on a methodical path to ace the Sentence Correction section on the GMAT.

In keeping with its exhaustive nature, this book is divided into five sections:

Section 1 - Gives you a quick overview of the basic grammar concepts   relevant to the GMAT.

Section 2 – Discusses the major error types tested on the GMAT

Section 3 – Covers minor errors, especially errors of usage, and confusing choices.

Section 4 – Provides you with a 125-question Practice Set to help you test your understanding of the concepts learnt in the SC Grail and your ability to apply those concepts on SC questions based on the GMAT pattern.

Section 5 – Provides a Quick recap of all the important concepts and rules covered in this book. This section saves you the trouble of taking notes so you can concentrate on understanding the concepts. Go through this section before every practice test that you take.

We have tried to make this book a one-stop solution for all your Sentence Correction needs. The book starts with a grammar review section so that you are conversant with the terms that will be discussed in latter parts of the book. English grammar is an extremely vast field but this section will focus only on those concepts that are relevant to your doing well on the GMAT SC section.

After the grammar review section the book will take you through the nine commonly tested errors on GMAT SC. Again the focus will be on discussing only those aspects of these errors that are known to have been tested on the GMAT. While 'Meaning' is relevant to every error type, we have added a separate chapter on *Meanings* just to highlight the fact that the GMAT is increasingly testing this particular aspect of sentences.

The GMAT also tests you extensively on the usage of certain terms such as *whether, such as, should, etc.* In fact we recently did a split of all the error types tested in the Sentence Correction chapter in OG 13 (you can download this report from the Free Resources section of our website) and 'Usage' featured among the top three error types tested in the OG 13. The third section of this book is dedicated exclusively to discussing the usage of commonly tested terms on the GMAT.

Once you have gone through the previous three sections, it is time to test how much of this you have actually absorbed. The 125 question practice set that makes up Section 4 of this book will help you do precisely that. These questions have been created in such a way that they will reinforce the important concepts again and again until you start getting them right.

We have noticed that students tend to forget important SC rules (such as when to use *that* and when to use *which*) when they take practice tests, as a result of which their verbal score goes down by several points. To resolve this problem we have added a fifth section to this book - the Quick Recall section. This section contains all the important SC concepts and rules in one place and we urge you to go through this section before every practice test that you take. You will see the benefit of this when you actually get down to doing SC questions in the test – your accuracy and speed both will improve considerably.

For most of the concepts covered in this book, you will also find an OG question reference that will provide you with the question number of similar questions present in the OGs 13 and 12. As a result, you can see how the concepts explained in this book are actually tested on the GMAT.

We have tried to make this book as comprehensive and, at the same time, as student friendly as possible. We hope you find this book useful in your prep.

Good Luck & Study Hard!

The Aristotle Prep Team

SECTION 1

Grammar Review

Grammar Review

Before taking a look at the specific errors that will be tested on GMAT Sentence Correction questions, it is important to brush up your basic grammar fundamentals. Many students ask us whether it is actually important to know such detailed grammar concepts. Well, for one the concepts covered in this chapter will be anything but detailed; we'll actually just be scratching the surface of English grammar. More importantly, you can choose to leave out these concepts in case you are targeting a score of around 600 but if your target is a 700+ score then you will need to have some basic idea of these concepts.

The idea behind this chapter is not to revisit the Wren & Martin but to get a basic comfort level with the different building blocks of a sentence.

So let's start by taking a look at the different parts of speech. These are basically the words that you use to make up a sentence. There are eight parts of speech in the English language:

1. Noun
2. Pronoun
3. Adjective
4. Verb
5. Adverb
6. Preposition
7. Conjunction
8. Interjection

1) Noun

Nouns are naming words. Everything we see or talk about is represented by a word which names it - that word is called a *noun*. Nouns can be names for people, animals, places, objects, substances, qualities, actions, etc.

> *i) Names for people, animals, places – Tom, Englishman, brother, cat, office, China*
>
> *ii) Names for objects and substances – chair, computer, hammer, oxygen, water, ice*
>
> *iii) Names for qualities – kindness, beauty, bravery, faith*
>
> *iv) Names for actions – rowing, cooking, reading, listening*

Common & Proper Nouns

A common noun is the word used for a class of person, place, or thing.

> *Examples: bus, man, town, steel, company, etc.*

A proper noun is the name of a particular or specific person, place, or thing. A proper noun always starts with a capital letter.

Examples: Alisha, Africa, Aunt Molly, Oscar Awards, BMW, etc.

Countable & Uncountable Nouns

A **countable noun** (or count noun) is a noun with both a singular and a plural form, and it names anything (or anyone) that you can count. You can make a countable noun plural and attach it to a plural verb in a sentence.

Countable nouns are the opposite of non-countable nouns and collective nouns.

In the following two sentences, the highlighted words are countable nouns:

*i) John painted the **fans** red and the **lamp shades** blue.*

*ii) The eucalyptus tree lost three **branches** in the **storm**.*

A **non-countable noun** is a noun that does not have a plural form and that refers to something that you could not usually count.

A non-countable noun always takes a singular verb in a sentence. Non-countable nouns are similar to collective nouns (though not the same), and are the opposite of countable nouns.

In each of the following sentences, the highlighted words are non-countable nouns:

*i) Living things cannot survive in the absence of **oxygen**.*

*ii) We decided to move the **furniture** from one room to another.*

In the above examples, the words *oxygen* and *furniture* cannot normally be made plural and take the singular verb *is* rather than the plural verb *are*.

Examples of Non-countable nouns:

- *love, happiness, information, news*
- *furniture, luggage, sugar, butter, water*
- *electricity, power, money*

Collective Nouns

A **collective noun** is a noun naming a group of things, animals, or persons. Even though it is possible to count the individual members of the group, you usually think of the group as one unit.

You need to be able to recognize collective nouns in order to maintain subject-verb agreement. A collective noun is similar to a non-countable noun, and is roughly the opposite of a countable noun.

*In each of the following sentences, the **highlighted** word is a collective noun:*

*i) The **pride** of lions spends most of its time sleeping. (The collective noun "pride" takes the singular verb "spends" and the singular pronoun "its")*

*ii) The **jury** has still not arrived at a verdict.*

*iii) The **army** is against the military ruler.*

List of some common Collective nouns

Army	Array
Audience	Band
Bevy	Board
Bunch	Cast
Choir/Chorus	Class
Committee	Corporation
Council	Crowd
Department	Faculty
Family	Firm
Group	Jury
Majority	Minority
Party	Public
School	Senate
Society	Staff
Team	Troupe

Possessive Noun

When you want to show that something belongs to somebody or something, add **('s)** to a singular noun and an apostrophe to a plural noun.

For example:

- *the student's pen (one student)*
- *the students' pen (two or more students)*

Noun used as an Adjective

As you know, a noun is a person, place, or thing, and an adjective is a word that describes a noun. Sometimes we use a noun to describe another noun. In that case, the first noun acts as an adjective.

Examples

- *Shoe rack*
- *Phone screen*
- *Tennis ball*

In some exceptional cases you can have several consecutive nouns acting as adjectives.

For example

- *Australian softball team*

In the above sentence *Australian* and *softball* are both nouns acting as adjectives modifying the final noun *team*.

To Sum it up:

- *Noun - the name of a person, place, or thing*

- *Common Noun – refers to a general group*

- *Proper Noun – refers to a particular item in a group*

- *Countable Nouns – can be counted (bottle, compters, etc.)*

- *Uncountable Nouns – cannot be counted (nitrogen, milk, etc.)*

- *Collective Nouns – group of items that are referred to in the singular (committee, family, etc.)*

- *Possessive Nouns – use apostrophe to show possession*

- *Nouns as Adjectives– race horse, cricket ball, etc.*

2) Pronoun

A **pronoun** is a word that is used to replace a noun or another pronoun in a sentence. You use pronouns such as *he, she, them, their, which, that,* etc. to make your sentence less cumbersome and less verbose.

> *For example,*
>
> *Do you like the CEO? I don't like the CEO. I think the CEO is too arrogant.*

The above lines sound wordy and repetitive. Using pronouns, we can reframe the above lines as:

> *Do you like the CEO? I don't like him. I think he is too arrogant.*

The first sentence sounds awkward while the second sentence replaces the second noun *CEO* with the pronouns *him* and *he* and gets the meaning across more crisply.

Singular & Plural Pronouns

There are several pronouns that seem to be plural but act as singular, taking singular verbs. The most common of these pronouns are *anybody, anything, each, either, everyone, everybody, nobody, not one,* etc. These pronouns must be followed by a singular verb.

> *i) Not one of the apples was (not 'were') ripe.*
>
> *ii) Everyone has (not 'have') completed the assignment.*

Relative Pronouns

A relative pronoun is used to introduce a relative clause. A relative clause is used to modify an antecedent (can be a noun, phrase, clause) i.e. these clauses tell you more about the antecedent.

> *For example: The man **who** met me yesterday is my uncle.*

In the above sentence, the relative pronoun *who* modifies the *man* and provides more information about him.

There are five relative pronouns used most commonly- *who, whom, whose, that, and which.* The compounds *whoever, whomever,* and *whichever* are also relative pronouns.

In each of the following sentences, the **highlighted** word is a relative pronoun.

    *i) You may invite **whomever** you like to the reception.*

    *ii) The student **who** scores the highest marks is not always the smartest.*

    *iii) The box, **which** was lying in the garage, has now been moved into the attic.*

Indefinite Pronouns

An indefinite pronoun, as the name suggests, does not refer to a specific noun. It is vague and not specific or definite. Examples include *all, any, some, anybody, everything, etc.*

1. ***Anyone*** *can come for the concert*

2. ***Everybody*** *enjoyed the game*

3. *Jack gave the book to **somebody***

4. *Can **anyone** help me with this question*

5. *I knocked several times but **nobody** answered*

There is an interesting characteristic of some indefinite pronouns that we'll cover in the chapter on **Pronoun errors** later in this book.

To Sum it up:

- ***Pronoun*** *– replaces a noun or another pronoun*

- ***All these are Singular*** *– everyone, each, not one, anybody, etc.*

- ***Relative Pronouns*** *– who, whom, whose, that, which*

- ***Indefinite Pronouns*** *- all, any, none, some, everything, etc.*

3) Adjective

An **adjective** modifies or describes a noun or a pronoun by describing, identifying, or quantifying words.

An adjective usually precedes the noun or the pronoun that it modifies.

In the following examples, the **highlighted** words are adjectives:

> i) The *red* balloon floated over the mountains
>
> ii) Mrs. Jones painted her **kitchen** walls in a **hideous** color
>
> iii) The **little** dog fought bravely with the **large** buffalo

An adjective can be modified either by an adverb or by a phrase or clause functioning as an adverb. In the next sentence, the adverb *unbearably* modifies the adjective *hot*.

> *Today is an unbearably **hot** day.*

Do keep in mind that it is possible for the same word to act as a noun, adjective, or verb in different sentences, depending on the context of the sentence. For example, in the next three sentences the word *model* is used as a noun, adjective, and verb respectively.

1. John is a *model* (noun)

2. John is a *model* citizen (adjective)

3. John *models* occasionally to earn some extra money (verb)

Comparative & Superlative Adjectives

We use comparative adjectives when talking about or comparing **two** things (not three or more things).

> *For example: Jack is **taller** than Peter*

A superlative adjective expresses the extreme or highest degree of a quality. We use a superlative adjective to describe the extreme quality of one thing in a group of things.

> *For example, Jack is the **tallest** of all my students*

We can use superlative adjectives when talking about **three or more** things (not two things).

Usually, we can get to the comparative form by adding *-er* at the end of a word and to the superlative form by adding *-est*.

To Sum it up:

- **Adjectives** – *tell us something about the noun*

- *They can be modified by adverbs*

- *The same word can act as a noun, adjective, and verb in different sentences*

- **Comparative** – *bigger*

- **Superlative** - *biggest*

4) Verb

The verb is perhaps the most important part of a sentence. The shortest sentence contains a verb. You can make a one-word sentence with a verb, for example:

"Run!"

You cannot make a one-word sentence with any other type of word.

Verbs are sometimes described as *action words*. This is partly correct because many verbs give the idea of action, of *doing* something. For example, words such as *speak, write, do, work*, all convey action.

However, there are some verbs that do not give the idea of action; they give the idea of existence or of a state of being. For example, verbs such as *be, exist, seem*, and *belong*, all convey state.

Thus, verbs are words that tell us what a subject **does** or **is** i.e. they describe:

- **action** (*Jack* **plays** *football*), or
- **state** (*Jack* **seems** *angry*)

In each of the following sentences, the verb or compound verb is **highlighted***:*

i) A tiger **bites** *its prey on the neck. (The verb* **bites** *describes the action the tiger takes)*

ii) In early September, Gordon **will start** *with his MBA Program. (Here the compound verb* **will start** *describes an action that will take place in the future)*

iii) The first book I read **was** *The Fountainhead, but I* **remember** *The Alchemist more vividly. (In this sentence, the verb* **was** *identifies a particular book and the verb* **remember** *describes a mental action)*

Helping & Main Verbs

Consider the following sentences:

- *I will*
- *People have to*
- *The Earth does.*

Do these convey any meaning to you?

Obviously not.

This is because these verbs are helping verbs and have no meaning on their own. They are necessary for the grammatical structure of the sentence, but they do not tell us much on their own.

We usually use helping verbs along with main verbs. They *help* the main verb. The sentences in the above examples are therefore incomplete. They need at least one main verb to complete them, as given below.

- *I will study.*
- *People have to eat.*
- *The Earth does rotate.*

Now the sentences definitely convey some meaning because the verbs that have been added are main verbs and have meaning on their own. They tell us something.

Transitive & Intransitive verbs

A transitive verb is one that must have an object to complete its meaning, and to receive the action expressed.

> *For example*

> > *John threw the ball. (the object **ball** is needed to complete the meaning of the sentence, hence **threw** is a transitive verb)*

An intransitive verb is one that is complete in itself, or that is completed by other words without requiring an object.

> *For example*

> > *John talked. (**talked** is an intransitive verb because it does not need a direct object to convey its meaning)*

Active & Passive Verbs

The Active voice is the normal voice that we speak in most of the time. In this voice the object receives the action of the verb performed by the subject.

Sounds complicated?

> *Look at this simple example:*

> > *Dogs eat bones.*

Here the subject *dogs* is performing an action *eat* on the object *bones*. Hence this sentence is in the Active voice.

As opposed to this, the Passive voice is less usual. In this voice the subject receives the action of the verb being performed by the object.

Let's modify the earlier example a little:

Bones are eaten by dogs.

Here the subject *bones* has an action *eaten* being performed on it by the object *dogs*. Hence this sentence is in the Passive voice.

Usually the Active voice has the construction *Who does What* (I read a book), while the Passive voice has the construction *What was done by Whom* (The book was read by me).

Verbs also have tense and mood connotations that will be discussed in subsequent sections of this book.

To Sum it up:

- **Verbs** – *express action or a state of being.*

- **Helping Verbs** – *Not enough on their own. Need the support of main verbs. E.g.- must, will, can, etc.*

- **Main Verbs** – *have meaning on their own*

- **Transitive Verbs** – *require an Object*

- **Intransitive Verbs** – *do not require an Object*

- **Active Voice** – *Who does What*

- **Passive Voice** - *What was done by Whom*

5) Adverb

An **adverb** can modify or describe a verb, an adjective, another adverb, a phrase, or a clause. An adverb indicates *manner, time, place, cause, or degree* and answers questions such as *how, when, where, how much, etc.*

While some adverbs can be identified by their characteristic *-ly* suffix, most of them must be identified by untangling the grammatical relationships within the sentence or clause as a whole.

- i) *The tailor **quickly** stitched the suit.* (In this sentence, the adverb **quickly** modifies the verb **stitched** and indicates in what manner (or how fast) the suit was stitched)

- ii) *The students sat **patiently** through the long lecture.* (In this sentence, the adverb **patiently** modifies the verb **sat**)

Apart from modifying verbs, adverbs can also modify adjectives and other adverbs.

For example:

- i) *The **seemingly** easy question stumped the students.* (In this sentence the adverb **seemingly** modifies the adjective **easy**)

- ii) *The trainer urged John to complete the exercise **more** expeditiously.* (Here the adverb **more** modifies the adverb **expeditiously**)

- iii) ***Unfortunately**, the shops are shut on Mondays.* (In this sentence, the adverb **unfortunately** modifies the entire sentence)

To Sum it up:

- *Adverbs – primarily modify verbs*

- *Can also modify adjectives, other adverbs, phrases, & clauses*

- *Usually end with '-ly'. E.g. slowly, quickly, etc.*

---

6) Preposition

A preposition is a word that links nouns, pronouns, and phrases to other words in a sentence. A preposition always goes with a noun or pronoun that is called the object of the preposition. Some common prepositions include *in, of, about, above, below, beneath, by, despite, down, and during.*

Examples:

- *The cup is **on** the desk.*
- *The cup is **under** the desk.*
- *The cup is **beside** the desk.*
- *He held the cup **over** the desk.*
- *He drank from the cup **during** class.*

In each of the preceding sentences, a preposition locates the noun *cup* in space or in time.

Prepositions will always come as part of prepositional phrases. A prepositional phrase always starts with a preposition and ends with a noun or a pronoun. A prepositional phrase can function as a noun, adjective, or adverb.

Examples:

- *I am going to stay **at home***
- *I reached the airport just **in time***
- *I got a present **from John***
- *John is going for a movie **with Terry***
- *The cat is sitting **under the table***

Ground Rule for Prepositions:

A preposition is always followed by a "noun". It is never followed by a verb.

A preposition cannot be followed by a verb. If you want to follow a preposition by a verb, you must use the *-ing* form which is technically a gerund, i.e. a verb in noun form (more on Gerunds later).

To Sum it up:

- **Prepositions** – *express a relation between parts of a sentence*

- *Must be followed by a noun*

- *E.g.: in, about, above, below, beneath, between*

7) Conjunction

Conjunctions are connecting words that are used to link words, phrases, and clauses.

Examples:

- *I ate the burger **and** the sandwich.*

- *Call the applicants **when** you are ready.*

Co-ordinating Conjunctions

Co-ordinating conjunctions *(and, but, or, nor, for, so, yet)* are used to join individual words, phrases, and independent clauses that are grammatically equal. There are seven such conjunctions which can be remembered using the acronym FANBOYS – *For, And, Nor, But, Or, Yet, So.*

Examples

- *BMW **and** Mercedes are German car manufacturers.* (In this example, the co-ordinating conjunction **and** links two nouns).

- *John did well on the GMAT **because** he studied very hard.* (In this example, the co-ordinating conjunction **because** is used to link two independent clauses)

Note: One can also use the conjunctions **but** and **for** as prepositions.

Subordinating Conjunctions

A subordinating conjunction introduces a dependent clause and indicates the nature of the relationship among the independent clause(s) and the dependent clause(s).

Note: Dependent & Independent clauses will be covered later in this section.

The most common subordinating conjunctions are *after, although, as, because, before, how, if, once, since, that, though, till, until, when, where, whether, and while.*

Examples:

- *After she got a job, Alice felt more independent.* (The subordinating conjunction **after** introduces the dependent clause **After she got a job**)

- *If the train departs on time, you will reach Georgetown latest by 6 p.m.* (the subordinating conjunction **if** introduces the dependent clause **If the train departs on time**)

Conjunctive Adverbs

Conjunctive Adverbs are used to show relationships such as cause and effect, contrast, comparison, etc. Conjunctive adverbs include words such as *however, therefore, thus, moreover, nevertheless, etc.*

There are some peculiar rules with regards to the use of punctuation along with conjunctive adverbs. We'll discuss these in the next chapter under the section **Run on Sentences**.

To Sum it up:

- *Conjunctions* – *connect different parts of a sentence*

- *Co-ordinating Conjunctions* – *connect parts that are grammatically equal. E.g.- and, for, nor, etc.*

- *Subordinating Conjunctions* – *connect a dependent clause to a main clause. E.g.: although, because, since, etc.*

- *Conjunctive Adverbs* – *used to show relationships. E.g.: however, therefore, moreover, thus, etc.*

8) Interjection

Hello!

That's an interjection.

Interjections are short exclamations such as *Oh!, Ah!, etc.* They have no real grammatical value but we use them quite often, usually more in speaking than in writing. An interjection is sometimes followed by an exclamation mark (!) when written.

Examples:

- *Ah!*
- *Alas!*
- *Hmm*
- *Ouch!*
- *Oh No!*

Note: Interjections are NOT tested on the GMAT.

Those were the 8 parts of speech. Now let's look at the parts of a sentence and a few other terms that you need to know.

1) Subject, Object, and Predicate

A lot of the explanations in English grammar start with the terms *subject*, *object*, and *predicate*, so it's important that you have a clear understanding of what these three terms refer to.

Subject is the person or thing who/which carries out the action of the verb. In other words the Subject is the noun to which the sentence's verb refers.

> *For example,*
> *The teacher is playing with the students.*

In the above sentence, the main verb is *playing*. This action is carried out by the teacher. So, the *teacher* is the Subject of the sentence.

The **object** is the person or thing upon whom/which the action of the verb is carried out.

In the example above, the action *playing* is being carried out on the students. Thus *students* is the Object of the sentence.

The **predicate** in a sentence tells us what a person or a thing does or did or what happened to a person or to a thing? A simple predicate consists of a verb, verb string, or compound verb.

The predicate must,

     i) Agree in number with the subject
    ii) Have the correct tense, and
    iii) Be in the proper voice (active or passive).

*Thus, in the above sentence, **teacher** is the subject, **students** is the object, and **is playing** is the predicate.*

As you must have realized, a predicate must have a verb, and a verb all by itself can also be a predicate. However, this does not mean that *predicate* and *verb* refer to the same thing as there are verbs that are not predicates, and there can be predicates that have much more in them than verbs.

Let's look at one last example to recap:

The dogs are destroying the furniture.

Subject – the dogs

Object – furniture

Predicate – are destroying

To Sum it up:

- *Subject – person or thing that carries out the action of the verb*

- *Object - the person or a thing upon whom or which the action of the verb is carried out*

- *Predicate - tells about what a person or thing does or did*

2) Phrases and Clauses

A **Phrase** is a group of words that makes sense, but not complete sense. It's a group of related words without a Subject or a Verb or both.

Examples (the words in *italics* are Phrases):

- I am *reading a book.*
- John is an *actor of high caliber.*
- Kevin has *a black Siamese cat.*
- The fire *in the theater* was not very severe.

A **Clause** is a group of words that contains both a Subject and a Predicate, but may not be able to stand on its own. The most basic kind of sentence consists of a single clause; more complicated sentences may contain multiple clauses, including clauses contained within clauses.

Examples (the words in italics are Clauses):

- The dinner, *which he made for us,* was delicious.
- I can't believe that *the cat ran out of the door.*
- *The girl is nice*

Types of Clauses – Independent & Dependent

If a clause can make complete sense on its own, it is called an **Independent Clause**. It does not need to be joined to any other clause because it contains all the information necessary to make a complete sentence.

Examples:
- *The food is hot.*
- *The street is wet.*
- *She reads very fast.*

Dependent Clauses cannot stand up on their own and depend on another independent clause to make sense.

Examples:
- *Although the student is leaving*
- *Because tomorrow is a Sunday*

The above sentences don't make any sense on their own; they only make sense when you add an independent clause to both of them:

- *Although the student is leaving, he will come back tomorrow.*
- *Because tomorrow is a Sunday, I will wash my car.*

To Sum it up:

- *Phrases are groups of words that do not contain a Subject or a Verb or both*

- *Clauses are groups of words that contain both a Subject as well as a Predicate*

- *Independent Clauses are complete sentences and can make sense on their own.*

- *Dependent Clauses are not complete sentences and need to be connected to other clauses to make sense.*

- *Phrases make up a Clause and Clauses make up a Sentence.*

3) Verbals - Gerunds, Participles & Infinitives

The term **Verbals** refers to words that are based on verbs but are not used as verbs; rather they are used as nouns, adjectives, or adverbs.

There are three types of Verbals – *Gerunds, Participles, and Infinitives*

Gerund

A gerund is a verbal that ends in *-ing* and functions as a noun. Since it functions as a noun, it occupies the same positions in a sentence that a noun ordinarily would, such as subject, direct object, subject complement, and object of preposition.

> *Examples:*

> - *Running is a good exercise.*

In the sentence above, **running** is used as a noun and not as a verb.

> - *My friends do not appreciate my singing.*

> - *My dog's favorite activity is sleeping.*

Notice that in the above sentences the actions of *running, singing and sleeping* never really take place (in which case these words would become *verbs*). These are just terms that are used to name the actions i.e. they are naming words, which are the same as nouns.

Participle

A participle is a verbal that is used as an adjective and most often ends in *-ing* or *-ed*. It has some features of verbs and some of adjectives, but it is most basically a type of *adjective*. Since it functions as an adjective, participle can only modify nouns or pronouns.

There are two types of participles: Present participles and Past participles.

Present participles usually describe what a thing does and **Past Participles** usually describe what was done to a thing.

Present participles typically end in *–ing* whereas Past participles end in *-ed, -en, -d, -t,* or *-n*, as in the words *asked, eaten, saved, dealt,* and *seen.*

> *Example*

> *She is buying a **talking** bird for her daughter.*

*In this sentence, **is buying** is the verb and **talking** is used as an adjective to modify the noun **bird**. Hence **talking** here is used as a present participle.*

*A **broken** clock stood on the mantelpiece.*

*In this sentence, **stood** is the verb in the past tense and **broken** is being used as an adjective to modify the noun **clock**. Hence **broken** here is used as a past participle.*

More examples:

- The *crying* baby had a wet diaper.
- *Shaken*, he walked away from the *wrecked* car.
- The *burning* log fell off the fire.
- *Smiling*, she hugged the *panting* dog.

Note: The words *present* and *past* in Present Participle and Past Participle do not refer to the present and past tenses. You can use a present participle in a sentence that is in the past tense and a past participle in a sentence that is in the present tense. For example, in the first sentence above - The **crying** baby had a wet diaper – *crying* is the present participle but the sentence is in the past tense *had*.

Infinitive

An infinitive is a verbal consisting of the word *to* plus a verb (in its simplest form) and functioning as a noun, adjective, or adverb. Infinitives are easy to locate because of their '*to + verb*' form.

Examples

- The children wanted *to eat* (direct object)
- His ambition is *to fly* (subject complement)
- John lacked the will power *to resist* (adjective)
- We must learn *to behave* (adverb)

Students often get confused between an infinitive—a verbal consisting of *to + verb*—and a prepositional phrase beginning with *to*, which consists of *to + a noun or pronoun* and any modifiers. The following examples will make this difference clear:

Examples

- ***Infinitives:*** *to run, to write, to become, to stand, to eat, to belong*

- *Prepositional Phrases:* to her, to the chairman, to my shop, to the mountains, to this student

How to decide between an Infinitive and a Participle

An infinitive is almost always used to show intention or desire, whereas a participle (specifically a present participle) is almost always used to show the result or effect of something.

Example:

- John drove his car at 150 miles an hour, **causing** an accident.

- John drove his car at 150 miles an hour **to cause** an accident.

In the first sentence the present participle *causing* expresses the result or effect of driving at 150 mph, whereas in the second sentence *to cause* clearly suggests that John drove his car at a particular speed with the intention of causing an accident.

(OG 12 – Q 30)

To Sum it up:

- *Verbals* – Words based on a verb but not used as one

- *Gerunds* – end with '-ing' and used as nouns

- *Participles* – act as adjectives

- *Present Participle* – ends with '-ing'

- *Past Participle* – ends with '-ed', '-en', '-d', etc.

- *Infinitives* – to + verb. Can function as noun, adjective or adverb

- Use Present participle to show effect and Infinitive to show intention

4) Punctuation

The GMAT does not usually test candidates on punctuations, except for the **colon** (:), the **semi colon** (;), and the **comma** (,).

Colon

There are two main uses for the colon in everyday writing.

The first use is when introducing a list, and the second is when introducing an explanation or an example.

Examples

- *I need to pick up a few things from my office: folders, staplers, and board pins.*
- *After several days of deliberation, the Board made its decision: it was going to sell the company.*

Incorrect usage

- *My favorite places to shop are: the mall, the local shopping center, and the Internet.*

You always require an independent clause before the colon.

Semicolon

The semicolon is primarily used to connect two Independent Clauses. Independent clauses are groups of words that can stand alone as complete sentences. When you have two otherwise complete sentences that you want to connect to form one long sentence, use a semicolon between them.

Example: This could be a solution; this could be another one.

If you put a comma where that semicolon is, you will end up with a *comma splice* (also called Run-ons) which is a grammar error. Sometimes, the second clause doesn't really look like a complete sentence, so you must watch closely.

Example: Twelve birds had originally arrived; only six remain.

Note: If there's a conjunction between the clauses *(and, but, etc.)* you don't need to use a semicolon to connect the two complete sentences. In that case, use a comma.

Example: This could be a solution, and this could be another one.

Comma

The GMAT will never test you on the correct usage of a comma, since there is lack of clarity amongst grammar experts themselves on this issue. However, the knowledge of the ways in which the GMAT uses the comma, can enable you to spot the subtle hints that such a construction may provide you with.

To separate non-restrictive modifiers

The comma is used to set off non-restrictive modifiers in a sentence. In case you aren't sure of what restrictive and non restrictive modifiers are, these will be dealt with in a subsequent chapter in this book.

Example: The third house, which has got automatic gates, is mine.

Cannot be used to join two independent clauses

As we saw earlier in the case of semi-colons, a comma cannot by itself be used to join two independent clauses. A semi-colon, full stop, or conjunction should be used instead.

Examples:

- *My uncle Tom is coming today, his wife is also coming* – **Incorrect**

- *My uncle Tom is coming today, and his wife is also coming* – **Correct**

- *My Uncle Tom is coming today. His wife is also coming* – **Correct**

- *My uncle Tom is coming today; his wife is also coming* - **Correct**

Use of a Serial Comma

The serial comma is the comma used immediately before a coordinating conjunction (usually *and* or *or*) preceding the final item in a list of three or more items.

Examples:

- *John, Terry, and Sylvia are coming for dinner (with the serial comma).*

- *We will go on Monday, Tuesday or Wednesday (without the serial comma).*

Opinions vary among writers and editors about the usage of the serial comma. Some experts believe that it can be omitted while some insist that it must be used. It goes without saying that the GMAT will never test you on this rule.

The reason we have mentioned the serial comma in this book is because the GMAT always uses the serial comma *(OG 13 – Q 21, 37, 54, etc.)*, but these questions contain other errors and are not testing a student on the use of the serial comma.

To Sum it up:

- *Use colons to introduce either a list or an explanation*

- *Use semicolons to connect two independent clauses*

- *Never use a semicolon and a conjunction together*

- *Comma cannot be used to join two independent clauses.*

SECTION 2

GMAT Sentence Correction Error Types

Sentence Correction – Major Error Types

In the last section, we covered the basic grammar concepts that make up a sentence. Now let's look at the various Sentence Correction error types that are tested on the GMAT.

The Sentence Correction section tests your knowledge of English grammar by asking you to choose, from five options, that one option which best conveys the correct meaning of the sentence. Among other things, you will be tested on grammar usage, sentence style, and idiom usage.

As discussed earlier, the GMAT is a standardized test, which means that the GMAT will only test you on certain types of questions and only on certain specific concepts within those questions. On Sentence Correction, this translates into nine major error types that are tested over and over again.

These error types are:

- Fragments & Run-ons
- Subject Verb Agreement
- Tense
- Pronoun
- Modification
- Parellel Construction
- Comparison
- Idioms & Style
- Meaning

How to Approach a Sentence Correction Question

The most important thing to remember in Sentence Correction is that you don't have to know every rule of grammar to answer the questions correctly. Therefore referring to the Wren & Martin will probably not be of much help.

The GMAT does not expect you to become another Shakespeare; it expects you to perform well under timed conditions. In fact, it is very likely that most experts of English would struggle on the GMAT because of the time constraints.

Timing is one of the key components of the test; you not only have to get the answers correct but you also have to do so within the stipulated time. Ideally, in Sentence Correction, you should take approximately 1 minute to answer each question.

Now if you were to actually read all the five options completely, this in itself would take you more than a minute. Also, by the time you reach the last option, you will have most likely forgotten what you had read in the first or in the second option. As a result, you will end up going back and forth, wasting precious time.

Remember this - *At any time in a Sentence Correction question, if you are reading all the five options completely, you are wasting your time. If any teacher or coaching class tells you otherwise, RUN. This strategy will get you in a lot of trouble.*

So what do we suggest?

Our point is that you should be able to arrive at the answer by reading just a few specific words across the five options; at times (and we'll see such questions later) you'll be able to arrive at the answer by reading just the first 3-4 words of each option.

This is the best (perhaps the only) way of approaching Sentence Correction questions. Most students struggle because they don't see it this way.

Here is our Golden Rule for Sentence Correction:

You ALWAYS read vertically; you NEVER read horizontally.

What does this mean?

Consider the following sentence:

Roger Federer is regarded to be the best tennis player on the planet.

Can you spot any errors in this sentence? If you can, then immediately eliminate all the options that contain that error. But what to do if you can't spot the error?

Given below is the same question along with five options. We want you to look at the first word of every option (only the first word) and group the options on this basis.

Roger Federer is regarded <u>to be the best tennis player on the planet.</u>

A)   *to be the best tennis player on the planet*
B)   *as the best tennis player on the planet*
C)   *as being the best tennis player on the planet*
D)   *to be the best tennis player in the planet*
E)   *as the best tennis player in the planet*

As you can see, two options start with *to* and three options start with *as*. Now, both of these cannot be correct, so depending on which one of these is correct you can eliminate either two or three options without reading another word in those options. This will save you valuable time, enabling you to finish the question in less than a minute.

In case you are curious, the answer to the above question is B;

- *'regarded as' is the correct idiom and not 'regarded to be', so eliminate A & D.*

- *'as being' in C is again idiomatically incorrect.*

- *the correct construction is 'on the planet' or 'in the world' not 'in the planet'. So E is out.*

You may not always be able to group the options using the first words; sometimes you can do this using the last words; sometimes you can do this using the error itself (assuming you have already spotted the error); sometimes you can do this using an idiom. What you need to ensure is that you are always reading vertically and eliminating options, rather than reading horizontally and wasting your time/getting confused.

*We have used this strategy to solve each of the Sentence Correction questions in the OGs 12 and 13. The same are available in our books – **Ultimate One-Minute Explanations to OG 12/13 SC.** Check these out if you haven't already.*

The "Aristotle Prep Sentence Correction Approach"

Step 1 – Read the sentence once and try to identify the error

Step 2 – If you can identify the error, eliminate all the options that contain that error

Step 3 – If you can't identify the error, group the options using the first or the last words (or in any other manner)

Step 4 – Eliminate until one option remains

Now that we have discussed the general approach to a Sentence Correction problem, let's take an in-depth look at each error that you will be tested on.

Very Important Tip:

Always pay attention to the non-underlined part of the sentence, especially if you get stuck between two options, both of which look correct. One mistake students often make is to just skim through the non-underlined part and focus only on the underlined part. There are numerous instances in the OG in which the answer can be arrived at quickly by looking at the part that is not underlined. This is especially true for *Tense* and *Parallelism* errors.

(OG 13 – Q 3, 8, 109, 132)
(OG 12 – Q 38, 124)

Fragments
&
Run-on Sentences

Fragments

Let's start by looking at what makes up a complete sentence:

Sentence = Subject + Verb/Predicate + Meaning

So to make a complete sentence you need three things – a subject, a predicate, and some meaning. If any of the three is missing, the sentence is called a fragment. Almost always it is the verb that will be missing in these sentences.

Consider the following example:

Bruce going for a movie today.

Does the sentence contain all three of the above requirements?

The subject is Bruce but what is the verb? *Going*?

Going by itself cannot act as a verb, it needs a helping verb such as *is* before it. Hence the correct sentence should read:

Bruce is going for a movie today.

(OG 13 – Q 1, 29, 45)

Fragment trap with Relative clauses:

A common way of confusing students with Fragments is by using relative clauses in a sentence. Consider the following two sentences:

1. *The book is lying on the table.*

2. *The book that is lying on the table*

Are both of these complete sentences or is one of these a fragment?

Sentence 1 – contains the subject *book*, the helping and main verbs *is lying*, and also conveys some meaning. So this is definitely a complete sentence.

Sentence 2 – contains the subject *book*, but does it contain a verb? Is *is lying* acting as a main verb in this sentence? If you read the sentence you will most likely think that the sentence appears incomplete and does not convey any meaning as such. This is because the relative clause *that is lying on the table* is describing the position of the book, but we require a main clause outside of this relative clause for the sentence to make sense. Hence this sentence is actually a fragment. The following can be one of way of correcting this fragment, but there can be several other ways as well:

The book that is lying on the table is mine

In the above sentence the main verb is the *is* before *mine* so now the sentence has a subject, a verb, and some meaning and hence is a complete sentence.

Run-on Sentences

A Run-on Sentence (sometimes also referred to as a comma splice or a fused sentence) is when you use a comma to connect two independent clauses. In case you've forgotten what independent clauses are (this was covered earlier in this book), these are clauses which contain a subject, a verb, and some meaning i.e. they can stand on their own.

Consider the following sentence:

Michael Phelps is a great swimmer, he has won 22 Olympic medals.

Is the above sentence correct? Specifically, is the use of the comma correct in the above sentence?

In this sentence, look at the part before the comma - *Michael Phelps is a great swimmer*. This contains a subject, verb, and meaning all three so this is an independent clause.

Again look at the part after the comma – *He has won 22 Olympic medals*. This is also an independent clause.

Keep in mind that you can never use a comma to connect two independent clauses. If you do so, such a sentence is called a run-on sentence or a comma splice. If you do away with the comma as well, then the sentence is called a Fused sentence.

So a run-on sentence is when you connect two independent clauses using an improper connecting word or punctuation, most often a comma.

(OG 13 – Q 124)

How to correct a Run-on Sentence?

There are four ways of correcting Run-on sentences:

1.   Use a full stop (.)

Michael Phelps is a great swimmer. He has won 22 Olympic medals.

2. Use a semi colon (;)

> *Michael Phelps is a great swimmer; he has won 22 Olympic medals.*

3. Use a coordinating (FANBOYS) conjunction

> *Michael Phelps is a great swimmer **and** he has won 22 Olympic medals.*

4. Use a relationship word to make one clause dependent on the other

> ***Because** Michael Phelps is a great swimmer, he has won 22 Olympic medals.*

Note: To correct a run-on sentence you use either a semi colon or a coordinating conjunction but not both. The following is an incorrect sentence;

> *Michael Phelps is a great swimmer; and he has won 22 Olympic medals.*

Run-on Sentences and Conjunctive Adverbs

We discussed the term *Conjunctive Adverb* earlier in this book under the topic **Conjunctions**. To quickly recap, conjunctive adverbs are connecting words such as *therefore, hence, thus, however, moreover, etc.*

The following punctuation rules need to be followed when using conjunctive adverbs in a sentence:

When a conjunctive adverb is used to connect two independent clauses, it must be preceded by a semi colon and followed by a comma.

Consider the following sentences:

1. *The athlete practiced very hard, therefore he won the race.*
2. *The athlete practiced very hard, so he won the race.*
3. *The athlete practiced very hard, but he lost the race.*
4. *The athlete practiced very hard, however he lost the race.*

Of these, sentences 2 and 3 correctly use the coordinating conjunctions *so* and *but* to connect two independent clauses.

However sentences 1 and 4 are incorrect, even though they may appear correct to you. This is because conjunctive adverbs always need to be preceded by a semi colon and not by a comma. The way they are written, sentences 1 and 4 are in fact run-on sentences.

The correct sentences will read:

1. *The athlete practiced very hard; therefore, he won the race.*

2. *The athlete practiced very hard; however, he lost the race.*

Note that the conjunctive adverbs *therefore* and *however* are also followed by a comma

When a conjunctive adverb is part of one single clause then it only needs to be set off by commas. A semi colon is not required in this case.

For example,

> *The CEO has suggested price cuts as a way to counter the increased competition. The Board, however, disagrees with him.*

In this sentence the conjunctive adverb *however* is not being used to join two independent clauses; hence, it is just set off by commas.

Fragments and Run-on Sentences Practice Drill

Go through each of the following sentences and try to identify the fragment or run-on errors in them. Once you have identified the error, also try to come up with some way of fixing the same. Some of the sentences may be correct as written i.e. they may have no error.

1. The increase in the incidence of crime can be attributed to the decrease in the number of security guards in the locality, more than 500 of them have left their jobs in the last three months.

2. John is a good student, so he will do well on the GMAT.

3. John is a good student, therefore, he will do well on the GMAT.

4. The Eiffel Tower was erected in 1889, it is one of the landmarks of France.

5. Some students decide to pursue their MBAs immediately after completing their undergrad while some others working for a year or two before doing so.

6. The Board of Directors suggests that the controversial product be withdrawn from the market, however, the CEO argues that the product has a loyal clientele in the market.

7. The tiger sitting by the lake in the middle of the forest and growling at the tourists.

8. The athlete had put in a lot of effort in his preparation prior to the competition, thus, it came as no surprise that he won all the races that he participated in.

9. The student who is always the first to arrive for the class and who always brings his laptop along with him.

10. The residents troubled by doubts about whether the mayor will live up to the promises he had made earlier.

11. While many teachers work at schools in addition to conducting private tuitions.

12. I offered him a ticket to Spielberg's new movie; a movie he had always wanted to see.

Fragments and Run-on Sentences Practice Drill – Explanations

1. *Error:* Run on sentence

   Explanation: *The part before the comma is an independent clause and so is the part after the comma. A comma cannot be used to connect two independent clauses.*

   Possible Corrections:

   - *Use a semi colon in place of the comma.*
   - *You can also make the second clause dependent on the first by replacing 'them' with 'whom'. In this case you don't need the semi colon, the comma will be fine.*

   ----

2. *Error:* No error

   Explanation: *The sentence correctly uses the coordinating conjunction so to connect two independent clauses.*

   ----

3. *Error:* Run on sentence

   Explanation: *This sentence uses the conjunctive adverb **therefore** to connect two independent clauses. In such cases the conjunctive adverb must be preceded by a semi colon and followed by a comma.*

   Possible Corrections:

   - *Instead of a comma, use a semi colon before 'therefore'*

   ----

4. *Error:* Run on sentence

   Explanation: *The part before the comma is an independent clause and so is the part after the comma. A comma cannot be used to connect two independent clauses.*

   Possible Corrections:

   - *Instead of a comma, use a semi colon before 'it'*
   - *Connect the two clauses using a FANBOYS conjunction such as 'and'*

   ----

5. **Error:** *Fragment*

    Explanation: *The sentence consists of two clauses – one before 'while' and one after 'while'. The clause after 'while' is missing a verb and hence becomes a fragment ('working' is a participle and not a verb).*

    Possible Corrections:

    - *Replace the present participle working with the verb work*

    ----

6. **Error:** *Run-on sentence*

    Explanation: *This sentence uses the conjunctive adverb **however** to connect two independent clauses. In such cases the conjunctive adverb must be preceded by a semi colon and followed by a comma.*

    Possible Corrections:

    - *Instead of a comma, use a semi colon before 'however'*
    - *Replace 'however' with a FANBOYS conjunction such as 'but'*

    ----

7. **Error:** *Fragment*

    Explanation: *The sentence is missing a verb such as **is** or **was**.*

    Possible Corrections:

    - *Insert the helping verb 'is' before 'sitting' – The tiger is sitting……and growling*

    ----

8. **Error:** *Run-on sentence*

    Explanation: *This sentence uses the conjunctive adverb **thus** to connect two independent clauses. In such cases the conjunctive adverb must be preceded by a semi colon and followed by a comma.*

    Possible Corrections:

    - *Instead of a comma, use a semi colon before 'therefore'*
    - *Replace 'therefore' with a FANBOYS conjunction such as 'so'*

    ----

9. **Error:** *Fragment*

    Explanation: *The sentence is missing a main verb. The two relative clauses starting with 'who' modify or describe the student but the main verb needs to come outside of these two clauses.*

    Possible Corrections:
    - *Remove both the 'who's' from the sentence making 'is' the main verb*
    - *Add a main verb at the end of the sentence – The student who is always the first to arrive......and who always brings his laptop along with him **has not come today**.*

    ----

10. **Error:** *Fragment*

    Explanation: *The sentence is missing a main verb. For 'troubled' to act as a verb, it needs to be preceded by a helping verb such as **is** or **are**.*

    Possible Corrections:
    - *Add a helping verb before 'troubled' – The residents **are** troubled by doubts about...........*

    ----

11. **Error:** *Fragment*

    Explanation: *This sentence contains a subject and a verb but is missing the meaning. The use of 'while' at the beginning of the sentence makes this a dependent clause but there is no independent clause in the sentence on which this dependent clause can depend.*

    Possible Corrections:
    - *Remove the 'while' making the clause an independent clause.*

    ----

12. **Error:** *Fragment*

    Explanation: *A semi colon is used to connect two independent clauses. In this sentence, the part after the comma is not an independent clause; rather it is an appositive phrase describing the noun before the comma i.e. Spielberg's new movie. Appositives do not lead to run on sentences.*

    Possible Corrections:
    - *Replace the semi colon with a comma.*

Subject-Verb Agreement

Subject-Verb agreement is the most basic of concepts in the English language. While conceptually it appears simple and straightforward, the GMAT has several ways of complicating things, as we will discover later in this chapter.

Subject-Verb Agreement Rule

A singular subject must take a singular verb and a plural subject must take a plural verb.

A subject is whatever is doing the action of the verb (For details, refer to the previous section of this book). A very simple example of a Subject-Verb mismatch could be the sentence:

The students has taken the test.

The singular verb *has* does not agree with the plural subject *students*.

So, the correct sentence should read:

*The **students have** taken the test (plural subject & plural verb)*
OR
*The **student has** taken the test (singular subject & singular verb)*

Now, let's look at a more GMAT-type question:

Recent studies indicate that the ability of a soldier to remain calm under attack by enemies, internal or external, <u>determine whether the soldier will be the victor or the vanquished.</u>

- A) *determine whether the soldier will be the victor or the vanquished.*
- B) *determines whether the soldier will be the victor and the vanquished.*
- C) *determine whether the soldier should be the victor and the vanquished.*
- D) *determines whether the soldier will be the victor or the vanquished.*
- E) *determine if the soldier will be the victor or the vanquished.*

Follow the "Aristotle Prep method", and look at the first word of every option. Ask yourself whether it should be *determine* or *determines*? Since it is the singular *ability* and not the plural *enemies* that determines, the correct option should be the singular *determines* (and no, adding an *s* to a verb does not make it plural; this actually makes it singular in most cases).

Analyzing the options

- *A, C, & E are out because of the plural **determine***

- *Between B & D, the correct choice has to be D because the **and** in option B distorts the meaning of the sentence. How can the soldier be both the victor and the loser?*

How will Subject-Verb Agreement be tested on the GMAT?

1) Placing the subject and the verb far away from each other

There are primarily three ways of separating the subject from the verb:

i) By using Appositives

Appositives are nouns, pronouns, or noun phrases that are placed next to nouns to further describe them. If you see large parts of a sentence separated by a comma, it might be a good idea to ignore the part between commas and read the rest of the sentence as a whole.

For example

Nuclear fusion, one of the most effective ways of separating carbon and oxygen atoms, are being used with deadly intent by some countries.

In this sentence, seeing the plural *are* next to the plural *atoms*, you could get tricked into thinking that the sentence is correct the way it is written. To avoid such confusion, omit the part between commas, and the error will immediately become obvious to you – how can *nuclear fusion* take the plural verb *are*? Thus the correct sentence will read:

Nuclear fusion, one of the most effective ways of separating carbon and oxygen atoms, is being used with deadly intent by some countries.

ii) By using Relative Clauses

The Spanish artist, who is one of the world's leading exponents of Salsa and is known to have taught thousands of students, are living in exile.

This is obviously incorrect, since the subject is the singular *artist* but the verb is the plural *are*. The sentence tries to confuse you by ending the relative clause with the plural *students*.

The correct sentence will read,

The Spanish artist, who is one of the world's leading exponents of Salsa and is known to have taught thousands of students, is living in exile.

(OG 13 – Q 107, 133)

iii) By using a Prepositional Phrase

The animals in the zoo is hungry.

In this sentence, the subject is the plural *animals*, so the verb must be the plural *are* and not the singular *is*. Remember, in case of a prepositional phrase (*in the zoo*), the subject is always before the preposition and NOT after it (exceptions to this rule are words used to express quantity that we will see later in this chapter).

The correct sentence will read,

The animals in the zoo are hungry.

(OG 13 – Q 3, 7)
(OG 12 – Q 2)

2) Confusing you with Additives

Look at the following two sentences:

   i.   *John, as well as his friend, is coming for dinner*
   ii.   *John, as well as his friend, are coming for dinner*

Which one do you think is correct?

Surprising as it may sound, if you have answered (ii) then you are wrong. (i) is actually the correct sentence. In English, only the word *and* can make a subject plural. All other phrases (such as *as well as* in the example above) merely add extra information to the subject. These phrases are called *additives*. When you use additives the subject always comes before the additive phrase.

Here is a list of some common additives:

- *in addition to*
- *along with*
- *as well as*
- *together with*
- *including*

So to sum up:

*John and his friend **are** coming for dinner.*
BUT
*John as well as his friend **is** coming for dinner.*

How about this sentence?

Strawberries and cream is/are a high calorie snack.

In this case, even though *and* is being used as the connector, the correct verb will be *is*. This is an exception to the above rule - If two words connected by the word *and* are thought of as a single unit, they're considered a singular subject.

A hint is to look at the word that follows the verb. If this word is singular, the verb most probably will be singular. For example, in the sentence above, the singular word *snack* follows *is* and this reinforces the conclusion that strawberries and cream is a singular subject.

(OG 13 – Q 6)
(OG 12 – Q 5)

3) Either or / Neither nor

A) *Neither John nor his friends are/is sleeping in the lobby.*

B) *Neither John's friends nor John are/is sleeping in the lobby.*

With *neither…..nor* and *either….or* constructions, you always **make the verb agree with the subject that is closer to it.**

So, in option A, the correct verb should be *are* (agrees with nearer subject *friends*), and in option B, the correct verb should be *is* (agrees with the nearer subject *John*). The same rule applies to *either…or* constructions as well.

Note: When *either* or *neither* is used in a sentence without the *or* or *nor*, then the verb has to be singular.

For example: *Neither of John's friends **is** here*

4) Collective Nouns

Collective nouns are almost always singular. So, a flock of sheep *is* grazing and not *are* grazing (flock is a collective noun).

There are some cases in which a collective noun can be plural but these will almost never be tested on the GMAT, so for GMAT purpose treat collective nouns as singular.

For more examples of collective nouns, check the previous section on Grammar review.

5) Each & Every

Each of the students (is/are) in the class.

If you have marked *are* as the correct option, you are wrong, because *each* is singular; so the correct verb should be *is*.

Here is a list of some other commonly confused singular subjects:

- *Each/Every*
- *Anyone/Everyone/Someone*
- *Anybody/Everybody/Somebody*
- *Anything/Everything/Something*
- *Whoever/Whatever*
- *Either/Neither (unless accompanied with 'or' in which case refer to previously discussed rule)*
- *Nobody/Nothing/No one*

6) The number / A number

The number is singular

> *The **number** of students standing outside the office **is** increasing.*

A number is plural

> *A **number** of students **are** standing outside the office.*

7) Expressions of Quantity

When discussing fractions or percentages, always get the verb to agree with the subject after the preposition. This is an exception to the preposition rule discussed earlier.

> For example,
>
> *Half of the **money is** stolen*
>
> but
>
> *Half of the **books are** stolen*

When discussing majority, remember that *majority* by itself is singular but when majority refers to a set of people it is plural.

For example,

- *A majority is always right.*
- *A majority of students are right.*

8) One of the X who/that Y...

Consider this sentence:

This is one of the cars that belong/belongs to him.

Which one do we go with, the singular *belongs* or the plural *belong*? The answer is the plural *belong*.

In general, remember the following structure for such sentences:

One of the Noun (will always be plural) + that/who + Plural Verb

Examples:

- *He is one of the students who study here.*
- *Any of the members who disagree may leave the committee.*
- *This is one of the questions that are incorrect.*

However, please do not confuse this construction with the one below:

*One of the chairs is broken (not **are broken**)*

The structure for such sentences is:

One of the Noun (will always be plural) + Singular Verb (usually 'is')

It is only when the plural noun is followed by 'that/who' that the singular verb changes into plural.

9) Inverted Sentences

Usually in a sentence the subject always precedes the verb, but sometimes the GMAT can reverse this order, so that the verb comes before the subject.

For example,

*Through the Golden Eagle Bridge **passes** thousands of vehicles every day.*

In the above sentence, the singular verb *passes* is not referring to the singular *Golden Eagle Bridge* but to the plural *thousands of vehicles*. Hence, the correct verb will be the plural *pass.*

*Through the Golden Eagle Bridge **pass** thousands of vehicles every day.*

10) Indefinite Pronouns

We have already discussed what indefinite pronouns are in the previous section of this book. While most indefinite pronouns are plural, there are a few that can be both singular and plural depending on the context.

These are – *all, none, some, any, most*

- *Some of the students are in the class*
- *Some of the water is in the glass.*

Tips for Subject Verb Agreement questions:

- If the sentence is very long, omit the part between commas
- Collective nouns are almost always singular
- Whenever you see the words *each, every, and, as well as, or, etc.* in a setence always, check for subject-verb agreement mismatch
- If you are still confused go with the singular
- *All, none, some, any, and most* can be both singular and plural

Subject-Verb Agreement Practice Drill

Go through each of the following sentences and try to identify whether the subject is singular or plural. Accordingly get the subject to agree with the correct verb form. Some of the sentences may be correct as written i.e. they may have no error.

1. Motorcycles and scooters has/have two wheels each.

2. Motorcycles or scooters has/have two wheels each.

3. Delivering pizzas or selling newspapers is/are not (a) glamorous job/jobs.

4. Each of the boys has/have two notebooks.

5. Each of the boys or girls has/have two notebooks.

6. Every teacher and student has/have to complete the assignment.

7. Popcorn and Pepsi is/are John's favourite snack.

8. Popcorn and Pepsi is/are John's favourite snacks.

9. Neither the actors nor the director was/were there on time.

10. Neither the director nor the actors was/were there on time.

11. Neither of the actors was/were there on time.

12. A group of students believes/believe that the park should be cleaned.

13. A majority of citizens is/are against the bill.

14. A number of books has/have been stolen from the library.

15. The number of books stolen from the library is/are increasing at an alarming rate.

16. Through the toll plaza cross/crosses thousands of cars everyday.

17. Jessica told her counsellor that either of the two courses was/were fine with her.

18. The gardens, along with the beautiful monuments, make/makes Madrid a beautiful city.

19. The CEO as well as the trainees is/are coming for lunch.

20. The trainees as well as the CEO is/are coming for lunch.

21. In this poorly designed building, there is/are a lack of parking space and an abundance of pillars.

22. The incidence of crime and petty theft in this county is/are increasing every year.

23. The simplest of errors go/goes unnoticed by most students.

24. Both the books and the pen is/are mine.

25. It is commonly stated that neither joy nor happiness last/lasts forever.

26. It is imperative that everyone contribute/contributes to this exercise.

27. One of the books is/are missing.

28. One of the books that is/are missing is mine.

29. Ten years is/are a long time to work at the same company.

30. In a car there is/are always a brake and an accelerator.

Subject-Verb Agreement Practice Drill – Explanations

The subject and verb have been highlighted for easy identification.

1. **Motorcycles and scooters** has/**have** two wheels each.

   Explanation: The plural subject 'motorcycles and scooters' requires the plural verb 'have'.
   ----

2. Motorcycles or **scooters** has/**have** two wheels each.

   Explanation: In such 'or' constructions the verb needs to agree with the subject closer to it i.e. 'scooters'. The plural subject 'scooters' obviously requires the plural verb 'have'.
   ----

3. Delivering pizzas or **selling newspapers is**/are not (a) glamorous **job**/jobs.

   Explanation: The subject is after 'or' i.e. 'selling newspapers', which is obviously singular and needs the singular verb 'is'.
   ----

4. **Each** of the boys **has**/have two notebooks.

   Explanation: The use of 'each' always requires the singular verb, in this case 'has'.
   ----

5. **Each** of the boys or girls **has**/have two notebooks.

   Explanation: The use of 'each' always requires the singular verb, in this case 'has'.
   ----

6. **Every** teacher and student **has**/have to complete the assignment.

   Explanation: Don't let the 'and' confuse you, the use of 'every' always requires the singular verb, in this case 'has'.
   ----

7. **Popcorn and Pepsi is**/are John's favourite **snack**.

   Explanation: The last word 'snack' should give you a hint that the two items 'Popcorn and Pepsi' are actually considered one single item in this sentence and hence requires the singular verb 'is'.
   ----

8. **Popcorn and Pepsi** is/**are** John's favourite **snacks**.

   Explanation: As in the earlier sentence, the last word 'snacks' implies that 'Popcorn' and 'Pepsi' are considered two different items and hence require the plural verb 'are'.
   ----

9. Neither the actors nor the **director was**/were there on time.

   Explanation: In 'neither....nor' constructions you get the verb to agree with the subject that is closer to it. Hence the singular subject 'director' requires the singular verb 'was'.

   ---

10. Neither the director nor the **actors** was/**were** there on time.

    Explanation: In 'neither....nor' constructions you get the verb to agree with the subject that is closer to it. Hence the plural subject 'actors' requires the plural verb 'were'.

    ---

11. **Neither** of the actors **was**/were there on time.

    Explanation: 'Neither' and 'either' by themselves are always singular and require the singular verb.

    ---

12. A **group** of students **believes**/believe that the park should be cleaned.

    Explanation: In the case of prepositional phrases, the subject is always before the preposition. In this sentence the preposition is 'of', making 'group' the subject. The singular subject 'group' obviously requires the singular verb 'believes'.

    ---

13. A majority of **citizens** is/**are** against the bill.

    Explanation: When majority is used to refer to a group of people (citizens), it requires a plural verb.

    ---

14. A **number** of books has/**have** been stolen from the library.

    Explanation: 'A number' is always plural and requires a plural verb.

    ---

15. **The number** of books stolen from the library **is**/are increasing at an alarming rate.

    Explanation: 'The number' is always singular and requires a singular verb.

    ---

16. Through the toll plaza cross/**crosses thousands** of cars everyday.

    Explanation: This is an inverted sentence in which the subject 'thousands' is coming after the verb 'crosses'. Obviously the plural subject 'thousands' requires the plural verb 'cross'.

    ---

17. Jessica told her counsellor that **either** of the two courses **was**/were fine with her.

    Explanation: *'Neither' and 'either' by themselves are always singular and require the singular verb.*

    ----

18. The **gardens**, along with the beautiful monuments, **make**/makes Madrid a beautiful city.

    Explanation: *'Along with' is an additive phrase and the subject is always before the additive phrase. Hence, the plural subject 'gardens' requires the plural verb 'make'.*

    ----

19. The **CEO** as well as the trainees **is**/are coming for lunch.

    Explanation: *'As well as' is an additive phrase and the subject is always before the additive phrase. Hence, the singular subject 'CEO' requires the singular verb 'is'.*

    ----

20. The **trainees** as well as the CEO is/**are** coming for lunch.

    Explanation: *'As well as' is an additive phrase and the subject is always before the additive phrase. Hence, the plural subject 'trainess' requires the plural verb 'are'.*

    ----

21. In this poorly designed building, there is/**are a lack of parking space and an abundance of pillars.**

    Explanation: *There are two characteristics of the building – a lack of parking space and an abundance of pillars. Since the two are connected using 'and', we have a compound or plural subject that requires the plural verb 'are'.*

    ----

22. The **incidence** of crime and petty theft in this county **is**/are increasing every year.

    Explanation: *The subject is before the preposition 'of'. The singular subject 'incidence' requires the singular verb 'is'.*

    ----

23. The **simplest** of errors go/**goes** unnoticed by most students.

    Explanation: *The sentence is not talking about multiple errors but the one that is the simplest thereby making the subject singular.*

    ----

24. Both **the books and the pen** is/**are** mine.

    Explanation: *The use of 'and' gives us a plural subject that requires the plural verb 'are'.*

    ----

25. It is commonly stated that neither joy nor **happiness** last/**lasts** forever.

    Explanation: *The singular subject 'happiness' requires the singular verb 'lasts'.*

    ----

26. It is imperative that **everyone** contribute/**contributes** to this exercise.

    Explanation: *The singular subject 'everyone' requires the singular verb 'contributes'.*

    ----

27. **One** of the books **is**/are missing.

    Explanation: *The subject is 'one' book i.e. singular, so we require the singular verb is.*

    ----

28. One of the **books** that is/**are** missing is mine.

    Explanation: *In this case the verb that agrees with the singular subject 'one' is the 'is' at the end of the sentence (before 'mine'). However, for the verb in question, the subject is the plural 'books', so we require the plural verb 'are'.*

    ----

29. **Ten years is**/are a long time to work at the same company.

    Explanation: *In this sentence 'ten years' is considered one single entity and hence requires the singular verb 'is'.*

    ----

30. In a car there is/**are** always **a brake and an accelerator**.

    Explanation: *A car has two things – a brake and an accelerator. Since the two are connected by 'and', we get a plural subject that requires a plural verb 'are'.*

Tenses

When it comes to Verb errors, the GMAT will test you on primarily two things – Subject Verb Agreement and Tense. We have already seen Subject-Verb agreement in the previous chapter; now let us take a look at Tenses.

Tenses are verb forms that tell you about the time period in a sentence i.e. when does the action take place in a sentence. They can at times indicate whether an action has been completed or whether it is still in progress. Common sense dictates that there can only be three time periods – the past, the present, and the future.

Accordingly we have three types of tenses:

- The Past Tense – *was, were, had, etc.*

- The Present Tense – *is, are, has, have, etc.*

- The Future Tense – *will, would, etc.*

There are four variations of each of these three tenses:

1. **The Simple Tense** - The simple tenses are used to show habitual or frequent actions, actions occurring at the moment, or to state generally accepted facts.

2. **The Continuous/Progressive Tense** - Verbs in Continuous Tenses always express actions that are in progress during the time framework indicated: present, past, future, or any of the perfect timeframes.

3. **The Perfect Tense** - The Perfect tenses are used to indicate the completeness of an action – completed in the past or at the present time, or will be completed by some time in the future.

4. **The Perfect Continuous/Progressive Tense** – The perfect continuous tense is used to denote actions that were repeated over a period of time in the past, are continuing in the present, and/or will continue in the future.

So altogether we have the following 12 tenses:

Simple Present	Present Continuous
Present Perfect	Present Perfect Continuous
Simple Past	Past Continuous
Past Perfect	Past Perfect Continuous
Simple Future	Future Continuous
Future Perfect	Future Perfect Continuous

While this may look like a lot of information, and many students indeed tend to get overwhelmed with tenses, the good thing for you is that the GMAT will not require you to identify the tense that a sentence is in. You'll just be tested on your understanding of the meaning of the sentence.

Consider the following sentences:

- *John has been coming for my classes since last year.*

- *John came for my classes last year.*

- *John will have been coming for my classes for one year next week.*

Now you may not be able to correctly identify the tense (from the list of 12 tenses on the previous page) that each of these sentences is in, but most of you can definitely understand the meaning each of these sentences is trying to convey.

The first sentence implies that John was coming for my classes in the past and that he is still coming (*Present Perfect Continuous Tense*), the second implies that John used to come for my classes in the past (*Simple Past Tense*) but does not come for my classes any more, and the third sentence implies that John has been coming for my classes in the past and he will continue coming for my classes in the future as well (*Future Perfect Continuous Tense*).

As long as you are able to understand this meaning, it doesn't really matter whether you can correctly identify the tenses, whereas if you can correctly identify the tenses but are unable to grasp the meaning, then you will struggle with Tense questions.

While there are several aspects to tenses, in this chapter we will be concentrating on those aspects that are frequently tested on the GMAT. This will primarily include the simple and the perfect tenses.

THE SIMPLE TENSES

1) The Simple Present Tense

The simple present tense is used to discuss permanent situations and how frequently an event takes place.

- *I like to read books*

- *The earth is round*

- *The bus leaves at 10pm*

2) The Simple Past Tense

The simple past tense is used to talk about actions that happened at a specific time in the past. You form the simple past of a verb by adding *-ed* at the end of a regular verb (irregular verb forms are different).

- *I saw a play yesterday.*
- *She washed her car this morning.*
- *Did you complete your assignment?*

3) The Simple Future Tense

The Simple Future tense has two different forms in English: *will* and *be going to*.

Use *will* to express a voluntary action or a promise,

- *I will send you the report when I get it.*
- *I will translate the email, so that Jerry can read it.*
- *I won't tell anyone your secret*

Use *be going to* to express a plan,

- *He is going to spend his holidays in Jamaica*
- *Who are you going to invite to the dinner?*

THE PERFECT TENSES

1) The Present Perfect Tense

Use the Present Perfect Tense to denote an action that happened at an unspecified time before now. You can also use the Present Perfect to describe your experience or to talk about change that has happened over a period of time.

FORM - [has/have + past participle]

- *You have seen that play many times.*
- *Have you seen that play yet?*
- *You have changed since the last time I saw you.*

2) The Past Perfect Tense

If a sentence involves two actions taking place in the past with one action taking place before the other, then use the past perfect tense to refer to the earlier action and the simple past tense to refer to the latter action.

FORM - [had + past participle]

- *You had studied French before you moved to London.*
- *She understood the movie only because she had read the book.*
- *You did well on the test because you had studied very hard*

(OG 13 – Q 1, 38, 72)

(OG 12 – Q 90, 139)

3) The Present Perfect Continuous Tense

This is used to denote an action that started in the past and continues into the present.

FORM - [has/have + been + present participle]

- *John has been waiting here for two hours*
- *They have been talking for the last hour*
- *Recently, I have been feeling really tired.*

4) The Past Perfect Continuous Tense

Use the Past Perfect Continuous Tense to show that something started in the past and continued until another time in the past.

FORM - [had + been + present participle]

- *They **had been talking** for over an hour before Tony arrived.*
- *She **had been working** at that company for three years when it went out of business.*
- *How long **had** you **been waiting** to get on the bus?*

How will Tenses be tested on the GMAT?

1. Put different time periods in a Logical Sequence

As discussed earlier, tense questions will test you on your understanding of the meaning of a sentence. It would be very simple if the GMAT were to give you sentences in one time period only. Of course the GMAT likes to complicate things by giving you multiple time periods in the same sentence.

The professor predicts that as students become more and more dependent on coaching classes in the coming years, <u>coaching institutes have been mushrooming</u> across the country.

A) *coaching institutes have been mushrooming*

B) *coaching institutes will mushroom*

C) *coaching institutes are mushrooming*

D) *coaching institutes should mushroom*

E) *coaching institutes will be mushrooming*

The first part of this sentence – *as students become* – is in the future tense because when will the students become dependent? Obviously in the future. To match this, the second part also needs to be in the future tense.

Hence Options A & C immediately go out.

Option D incorrectly uses *should* to imply that the professor wants these coaching institutes to mushroom.

Between Options B & E, option E unnecessarily uses the future continuous tense *will be mushrooming*. Since the first part of the sentence is in the simple future tense, the second part should also be in the simple future tense, making B the correct answer.

On Tense questions it is very important that you pay attention to the part of the sentence that is not underlined because only then will you be able to grasp the overall meaning of the sentence.

(OG 13 – Q 5, 10, 38, 40, 77)

2. Choose between Simple and Perfect tenses

While choosing between the simple and perfect tenses, avoid the perfect tense as much as possible.

For example,

- *Dinosaurs had roamed the earth billions of years ago. (Past Perfect Tense)*
- *Dinosaurs roamed the earth billions of years ago. (Simple Past Tense)*

Since the sentence only speaks about one event in the past, you don't really require the past perfect tense; go with the simple past tense instead.

Of course in some cases the Perfect Tense may be required to clarify the sequence of events. For example,

- *Christie understood the book only because she had studied Mandarin.*
- *Christie understood the book only because she studied Mandarin.*

In this sentence the two events are taking place at different time periods. Christie had studied mandarin first and she understood the book later. Hence we require the past perfect tense with the earlier event. **So use the past perfect tense to indicate that an action took place before another action in the past.**

Now let's look at an interesting sentence:

- *Before John won the lottery, he was a poor locksmith.*
- *Before John won the lottery, he had been a poor locksmith.*

This sentence talks about two things in the past,

One – *John won the lottery*
Two – *John was a poor locksmith*

Since John was a poor locksmith before he won the lottery, the two things are taking place at different time periods. Hence the thing that took place earlier (was a poor locksmith) will take the past perfect tense *had* and the thing that took place later (won) will take the simple past tense *won*. Thus the second sentence will be correct.

However, the first sentence is also correct in this case. This is because the use of *before* makes the sequence of events absolutely clear. So if the sequence of events is obvious in a sentence (by use of words such as *before, after,* etc.) you do not need the past perfect tense. Needless to say the GMAT will almost never ask you to choose between two options based only on this difference. There will be some other error as well in one of the two options.

(OG 13 – Q 89)

3. Choose between Simple and Continuous tenses

The continuous tense is used to highlight the ongoing nature of an activity. On the GMAT, avoid the continuous tense as much as possible.

Supercell, a continuously rotating updraft deep within a thunderstorm, is not visible in all thunderstorms <u>because they require</u> very high wind velocity and moisture.

- A) *because they require*
- B) *because they will require*
- C) *because it will require*
- D) *because it requires*
- E) *because it is requiring*

In this sentence options A & B get eliminated because the plural *they* cannot refer to the singular *Supercell*.

Option C unnecessary uses the future tense *will* to refer to a fact.

Between Options D & E, avoid the continuous tense *is requiring* in E because this only refers to the current action whereas we are making a general statement of truth about Supercell; hence the simple present tense in **D should be the correct answer.**

4) Use of *has had* and *had had*

While students often get confused in the usage of these constructions, both of these are nothing but the present perfect and past perfect forms of the verb 'to have'.

- *Has/Have had - Present perfect of 'to have'*
- *Had had - Past perfect of 'to have'*

Look at the following sentence as an example:

John travels to many different countries.

The verb in the sentence above is *travels,* which is in the simple present tense. Now if we were to convert this sentence into the Present perfect tense, we need to add *has/have* followed by the past participle form of the verb (in most cases just add the words *-ed* to the verb, like *traveled* in the above sentence).

The final sentence would read something like this:

John has traveled to many different countries.

Similarly, to convert this sentence into the Past perfect tense (two actions happening in the past - the earlier action takes the past perfect and the latter action takes the simple past tense), we need to add *had* followed by the past participle form of the verb.

The final sentence would read something like this:

John had traveled to many different countries before he decided to settle down in New Zealand

Sounds fairly simple, but the problem starts when the verb in question happens to be *to have/has* instead of say *travels* in the above example.

For example, consider the following sentence:

Tim has several passenger cars

The verb in the above sentence is *has* and it is in the simple present tense. Now to convert this into the present perfect tense apply the rule as discussed above - *has* followed by the past participle of *has* which is *had.*

The final sentence reads:

Tim has had several passenger cars

Similarly, the past perfect tense will read - *had* followed by the past participle of *has,* so you get:

Tim had had several passenger cars before he decided to buy a sports car

So there are two things happening in the past - Tim had several passenger cars first, which takes the past perfect tense with the extra *had* and he *decided* (simple past tense) to buy a sports car later.

5) The *If.....Then* construction

Such a construction usually refers to a conditional statement in which the taking place of something depends on the taking place of something else. Such statements are mostly hypothetical in nature.

For example: *If it rains today, (then) I will carry an umbrella.*

Such sentences will always have two clauses – the **If** clause and the **Then** clause. The tense of the **Then** clause depends on the tense of the **If** clause. This gives rise to the following three possibilities:

IF Clause	*THEN* Clause
PRESENT TENSE If you **exercise**	WILL + Base Verb you **will become** healthy
PAST TENSE If you **exercised**	WOULD/COULD + Base Verb you **would become** healthy
PAST PERFECT TENSE If you **had exercised**	WOULD/COULD + Have + Past Participle you **would have become** healthy

There can be only three possibilities for the *If* clause as described in the chart above and, depending upon the same, you can arrive at the correct construction of the *Then* clause.

Tenses Do's and Don'ts:

Here's a quick checklist of what to avoid and what to go with, as far as Tenses are concerned:

- Make sure you read the given sentence completely before taking a look at the options. Pay extra attention to the part that is not underlined because this part may tell you which tense to go with in the underlined part of the sentence.

- Avoid the continuous tense *(-ing)* as much as possible. Constructions such as *am coming, have been coming, etc.* are rarely ever correct on the GMAT.

- Do not use the present continuous tense to refer to future events; instead use the simple future tense:

    Incorrect: *Barry is going on a cruise next month*

    Correct: *Barry will go on a cruise next month*

Tense Practice Drill

In each of the following sentences, identify the correct form of the verb (given in brackets) that can be inserted in the blanks. Some sentences may have more than one correct answer.

1. The dish I had yesterday is one I _____ (have) for many years now.

2. By the time the police _____ (arrive), the miscreants _____ (leave).

3. In one of the worst plane crashes ever, a passenger airplane _____ (crash) less than ten miles from the city yesterday.

4. John _____ (was) an ordinary door-to-door salesman before he _____ (become) the famous painter.

5. Alan _____ (has) a heavy breakfast, so he _____ (decide) to skip lunch.

6. Alan _____ (has) his breakfast when the bell _____ (ring).

7. The number of books in the library _____ (increase) by at least fifty percent by the time the renovation finishes next year.

8. The Alpaca _____(is) native to South America and _____ (is) introduced in North America in the 1950s.

9. The Dodo, a duck-like bird that _____ (become) extinct in the 1600s, _____ (is) native to Mauritius.

10. The teacher said, "If you study hard, you _____ (will/would) do well in the exam."

11. The teacher said that if I studied hard, then I _____ (will/would) do well in the exam.

12. Over the last several decades, the IT-enabled services business _____ (grow) into a multimillion-dollar industry.

13. Between 1990 and 2000, the IT-enabled services business _____ (grow) into a multimillion-dollar industry.

14. The IT-enabled services business _____ (grow) into a multimillion-dollar industry before the dot com bubble burst in 2002.

Tense Practice Drill – Explanations

1. **Correct Answer:** The dish I had yesterday is one I **have had** (have) for many years now.

   Explanation: Use the present perfect tense 'have had' to refer to an event that was true in the past and is also true now.

   ----

2. **Correct Answer:** By the time the police **arrived** (arrive), the miscreants **had left** (leave).

   Explanation: The sentence talks about two events in the past – the police arrived later and the miscreant left earlier. So use past perfect tense with the earlier action 'had left', and the simple past tense with the latter action 'arrived'.

   ----

3. **Correct Answer:** In one of the worst plane crashes ever, a passenger airplane **crashed** (crash) less than ten miles from the city yesterday.

   Explanation: Use the simple past tense 'crashed' to refer to a completed action in the past.

   ----

4. **Correct Answer:** John **was/had been** (was) an ordinary door-to-door salesman before he **became** (become) the famous painter.

   Explanation: Since the sentence talks about completed actions, we need to go with the past tense 'became' (John has already become the famous painter). For the first blank, while some of you may be tempted to use the past perfect tense 'had been', the simple past tense 'was' is also correct because the use of 'before' in the sentence makes the sequence of events clear. So both the simple past tense and the past perfect tense can be used for the first blank.

   ----

5. **Correct Answer:** Alan **had had** (has) a heavy breakfast, so he **decided** (decide) to skip lunch.

   Explanation: Since Alan had his breakfast first and skipped his lunch later, you need to use the past perfect tense with the earlier event (had had) and the simple past tense with the latter event (decided). It is also possible to put the earlier event in the simple past tense (had) and the latter event in the present perfect tense (has decided).

   ----

6. **Correct Answer:** Alan **was having** (has) his breakfast when the bell **rang** (ring)

    Explanation: This sentence emphasizes the ongoing nature of an activity. Alan was doing something when something else happened. Hence we need to use the continuous tense 'was having'.

    ----

7. **Correct Answer:** The number of books in the library **will have increased** (increase) by at least fifty percent by the time the renovation finishes next year.

    Explanation: The sentence states that an event will be completed at a particular time in future. Hence you require the future perfect tense 'will have increased'.

    ----

8. **Correct Answer:** The Alpaca **is** (is) native to South America and **was** (is) introduced in North America in the 1950s.

    Explanation: This is a tricky sentence and you might be tempted to use the past perfect tense in the first blank. This is where the meaning aspect of tenses comes into the picture. Can nativity ever be in the past? Of course not. Once a native always a native, so use the present tense with 'native'. Since the other event 'introduction' took place in the past, use the simple past tense 'was' with this.

    ----

9. **Correct Answer:** The Dodo, a duck-like bird that **became** (become) extinct in the 1600s, **was** (is) native to Mauritius

    Explanation: This is the exception to the earlier question. The only situation in which you can use past tense with 'native' is when the species has become extinct. Hence both the blanks in this case will be in the simple past tense.

    ----

10. **Correct Answer:** The teacher said, "If you study hard, you **will** (will/would) do well in the exam."

    Explanation: Since the 'If' clause contains the present tense 'study', the 'Then' clause will take 'will'.

    ----

11. **Correct Answer:** The teacher said that if I studied hard, then I **would** (will/would) do well in the exam.

   Explanation: Since the 'If' clause contains the simple past tense 'studied', the 'Then' clause will take 'would'.

   ----

12. **Correct Answer:** Over the last several decades, the IT-enabled services business **has grown** (grow) into a multimillion-dollar industry

   Explanation: Remember the use of the phrase 'over the last several decades' implies that the action or the effect of the action is true even in the present. So you need the present perfect tense 'has grown' in the sentence.

   ----

13. **Correct Answer:** Between 1990 and 2000, the IT-enabled services business **grew** (grow) into a multimillion-dollar industry

   Explanation: Since this sentence talks about a completed event in the past, it requires the simple past tense 'grew'.

   ----

14. **Correct Answer:** The IT-enabled services business **grew/had grown** (grow) into a multimillion-dollar industry before the dot com bubble burst in 2002.

   Explanation: Since the sentence talks about events in the past, we need to go with the past tense. Since the industry had grown first and the bubble burst later, we need the past perfect tense 'had grown' with the earlier event.

Pronouns

A pronoun is a word that replaces a noun in a sentence such as *he, she, it, they, their, etc.* The GMAT will test you on three aspects of Pronouns:

1. Pronoun Reference
2. Pronoun Agreement
3. Pronoun Case

1) Pronoun Reference

Ideally in a sentence a pronoun should refer to only one noun. If it is possible that a pronoun may refer to more than one noun, then ambiguity creeps into a sentence.

John and Jack went jogging and he fell down.

Who fell down, *John or Jack*? This is a classic case of Pronoun reference error. Either of the following options can correct this:

- *John and Jack went jogging and they fell down.*
- *John and Jack went jogging and John (or Jack) fell down.*

A pronoun refers to more than one noun

Sometimes a sentence is structured in such a manner that a pronoun can refer to more than one noun and, as a result, the reader is confused about the author's intentions.

Incorrect: *John encouraged Jerry to start a pest control business because **he** felt that the residents of the city would be willing to pay for the same.*

Who does *he* refer to, John or Jerry?

Correct: *John encouraged Jerry to start a pest control business because **John** felt that the residents of the city would be willing to pay for the same.*

(OG 13 – Q 69, 78, 107, 113)

A pronoun has no antecedent

In the earlier scenario, a pronoun was referring to more than one noun, whereas in this case a pronoun is mentioned in a sentence without a corresponding noun being mentioned anywhere.

Incorrect: *Despite the Board of Governors supporting the measure, **they** keep voting against it.*

The problem in this case is *they*. *They* obviously cannot refer to the *Board* because *Board* is singular and, more importantly, when the Board is supporting the measure why will it keep voting against the measure?

Correct: *Despite the Board of Governors supporting the measure, **the shareholders** keep voting against it.*

In some questions you might think it is very clear what or who the pronoun is referring to. Still, if there is an option that replaces this pronoun with a noun, go with that option.

For example:

> *The residents association informed the civic agency that it was getting the park cleaned.*

If you read this sentence, you might think that the pronoun *it* clearly refers to the *residents association*, but to another person *it* could very well be referring to the *civic agency*. Hence the ambiguity!

So, the suggestion is to **AVOID** pronouns in the correct answer choice as much as possible, especially if the pronoun comes at the end of a sentence. You can even use pronouns to do a vertical split of the options and first look at only those options that do not contain pronouns at all.

However do keep in mind that this is not exactly a grammar error; it's more of a logical one. The thing is sometimes the GMAT can give you questions in which all the options contain pronouns, some of which may be ambiguous. In such cases go with the option that is the least ambiguous.

For example, if you look at SC Q 8 in OG 13 (pg. 673), the use of *them* in the correct answer E looks very ambiguous because *them* could refer to *chambers* or to *tourists*. However since all the other options contain errors, you go with E.

2) Pronoun Agreement

Pronoun Agreement is conceptually very similar to subject verb agreement. When replacing a noun with a pronoun in a sentence, make sure the pronoun matches the noun in terms of singular and plural forms. You cannot replace a singular noun with a plural pronoun and vice versa.

> The **players** said that **he** can't come for practice.

The plural noun *players* cannot be replaced with the singular pronoun *he*. The correct sentence should read:

> The **players** said that **they** can't come for practice.

(OG 13 – Q 7, 8, 80, 90, 93)

3) Pronoun Case

Noun or Pronoun *case* refers to a pronoun's function in a sentence. There are three cases when it comes to pronouns:

i. **Subject Case** – The pronoun is used as a subject, E.g: I, he, they, who, etc.

ii. **Object Case** – The pronoun is used as an object, E.g: me, him, them, whom, etc.

iii. **Possessive Case** – The pronoun expresses ownership, E.g: my, mine, hers, theirs, whose, etc.

Pronoun Case in Compound Structures

In compound structures i.e. structures in which you have a noun and pronoun together, drop the other noun to determine which case to go with.

For example

- *The coach punished Debbie and **me/I***

- *Debbie and **me/I** were punished by the coach.*

In case of confusion, just drop *Debbie* from both the sentences and see which version of the pronoun makes more sense.

In the first sentence *The coach punished **I*** makes no sense whereas *The coach punished **me*** does; hence, go with *me*. Similarly in the second sentence go with *I*.

Possessive Pronouns can refer to Possessive nouns only

The senator's proposal has been criticized by his opponents.

In this sentence, the possessive pronoun *his* can correctly refer back to the possessive noun *senator's*.

The senator's proposal has been criticized by his opponents who call him shortsighted and inflexible.

In this sentence, the possessive pronoun *his* still correctly refers back to the possessive noun *senator's*; however, the objective pronoun *him* cannot refer back to the possessive *senator's*. The correct sentence should read:

The senator's proposal has been criticized by his opponents who call the senator shortsighted and inflexible.

4) The usage of *That* and *Which*

On GMAT Sentence Correction questions, you will frequently be asked to choose between *that and which*. Both these terms belong to a small group of words known as relative pronouns, which are used to relate parts of a sentence to one another.

Consider these two sentences

- *The fifth car, which is black in colour, belongs to Jack.*
- *The fifth car that is black in colour belongs to Jack.*

Are both of these sentences referring to the same car? Not necessarily.

The first sentence is definitely referring to the fifth car and we are provided with the additional information that it is black in colour, but even without this information we can easily identify the car because it has to be car number five.

The second sentence just takes you to the fifth black car; now this car could be the fifth car (in case the first four cars are also black) or it could be the tenth car or the twentieth car; in fact, it can be at any number as long as it satisfies the criterion of being the fifth black car.

So, on the GMAT, *which* is only explanatory or non-restrictive and is not needed to identify the subject of the sentence. In fact, you can easily remove the phrase starting with *which* and yet the meaning of the sentence would remain unchanged, whereas *that* is necessary to identify the subject of the sentence and cannot be done away with.

To make it even easier, remember the following two rules for *which* to be correct on the GMAT:

1. ***Which** should always come after a comma*
2. ***Which** must refer to the noun that comes immediately before the comma.*

In case, either of these conditions is not satisfied, there's a pronoun error in the sentence and needs to be corrected.

For example, let's modify the earlier example a little:

The fifth car in the row, which is black in colour, belongs to Jack.

Now even though *which* is coming after a comma, the noun immediately before the comma is *row*, but *which* refers to the *black car* and not to the *black row*. Hence, there is a pronoun error in the sentence since *which* has an incorrect referent.

The only **exception to the above rule** is when *which* is preceded by a preposition such as *in which, of which, from which, etc.* In such cases you do not need a comma before *which*

For example,

The group of which I am a member has been dissolved

In this sentence, even though there is no comma, the use of *which* is correct since it follows the preposition *of*.

(OG 13 – Q 8, 12, 48, 67, 87, 105, 106, 129)
(OG 12 – Q 10, 63, 66, 70, 71, 86, 104, 129)

Important: While the *which* rule will work on 99% of the questions, it is possible to have that rare question in which *which* does not refer to the noun immediately before the comma. Refer to OG 13 Question no. 29. However, note that in this question there is absolute clarity that *which* can only refer to *letters* because *which* cannot refer to *humans* and also because *which* takes the plural verb *were*.

(OG 13 – Q 29)
(OG 12 – Q 26)

5) The usage of *Who* and *Whom*

The difference between *who* and *whom* is exactly the same as the difference between *I and me, he and him, she and her, etc.*

Who, like I, he, and she, is a subject - it is the person performing the action of the verb. *Whom*, like me, him, and her, is an object - it is the person to/about/for whom the action is being done.

Consider the following two examples:

1. *Who is going for the movie?*

2. *Whom is this movie about?*

In sentence 1, *who* is the subject performing the action *going* on the object *movie*. In sentence 2 *movie* is the subject and *whom* is referring to the object of the sentence.

Author's Tip: Remember that if the answer to Who/Whom is I, he, she, etc., then the correct word is **Who** and if the answer is me, him, her, etc, then the correct word is **Whom**.

For example, in Sentence 1 discussed above, the answer to the question is *he* is going for the movie and not *him* is going for the movie. Hence, the correct word is *Who*.

Similarly, in Sentence 2, the answer to the question is the movie is about *him* and not the movie is about *he*. Hence, the correct word is *Whom*

Whom is also the correct choice after a preposition: *with whom, one of whom, etc.* and not *with who, one of who, etc.*

Important – *On the GMAT **who and whom** are used to refer to **people** and **that and which** are used to refer to **inanimate things**. However **whose** can be used to refer to both animate as well as inanimate subjects.*

(OG 11 – Q 89)

6) *Do it* vs. *Do so*

Consider the following question:

> *Although it is conceivable that man may someday be able to fly, there is no clear evidence at the moment <u>of his ability to do it</u>.*

> A) of his ability to do it

> B) of his doing that

> C) to do so

> D) that he can do so

> E) of his ability to do that

While Option A, B and E might look correct to some of you, the pronouns *it* and *that* are considered ambiguous by the GMAT since it is not clear what these pronouns refer to. In such questions the best option is to replace these pronouns with *so*.

This brings us to options C & D but C distorts the meaning by suggesting that evidence is doing something.

The correct answer, therefore, is D.

Author's Tip: *When stuck between **do it** and **do so**, always go with **do so**.*

7) One vs. You

Usually, when giving advice to others or while making general statements, we tend to use the pronouns *one* and *you*. Care must be taken never to mix up these two pronouns.

> **Incorrect:** *If one does not study, you should not be surprised when you do badly in the test.*

> **Correct:** *If one does not study, one should not be surprised when one does badly in the test.*

> **Correct:** *If one does not study, he or she should not be surprised at having done badly in the test.*

8) That vs. Those

> *The average scores of students this year are higher than that of students last year.*

When you get a question on the GMAT that is similar to the one above, you'll immediately assume you are being tested on Comparisons and check whether the comparison makes logical sense. Since you are aware that a common trick in such questions is to compare the average scores with students, you'll immediately scan the answer choices that do so and remove them (and this is the right approach, by the way).

However, in checking for Comparisons, you might forget to check for Pronoun Agreement. The moment you see *that* (as in the above sentence) you'll think it refers back to the scores, so the sentence is correct. However *that* cannot refer to a plural noun, it can only refer to singular nouns. To replace plural nouns you must use *those*. So the correct sentence will read:

> *The average scores of students this year are higher than those of students last year.*

Important: In the above sentence, *that* is being used as a demonstrative pronoun i.e. a pronoun that substitutes for a noun. In such cases *that* can never be plural. However when *that* is used as a relative pronoun, then it can easily modify plural nouns as well.

For example,

> *The books that are lying on the table belong to me.* (**that** is a relative pronoun modifying the plural noun **books**)

This sentence should make things clear for you:

> *The books that are lying on the table belong to me, but ~~that~~ those on the chair belong to Jerry.*

9) A Pronoun cannot refer to an Adjective

A pronoun, by definition, is meant to stand in place of a noun only. A common trick the test makers use it to confuse you between nouns and nouns that function as an adjective.

> *After the success of the Spanish football team in recent years, more and more people in Spain are taking it up as a sport.*

In the above sentence *Spanish* and *football* are both used as adjectives to modify the noun *team*. So the use of *it* (taking it up as a sport) is incorrect because *it* technically does not have a noun antecedent in the sentence.

The correct sentence should read:

> *After the success of the Spanish football team in recent years, more and more people in Spain are taking up football as a sport.*

Pronoun Practice Drill

Check each of the following sentences for errors of Pronoun Reference, Agreement, and Case, and also try to come up with the correct sentence. Some sentences may be correct as written.

1. Ever since the author criticized his publisher, he has been disliked by the masses.

2. The foreign delegation was greeted warmly by the mayor who presented them with a report on the development projects underway in the city.

3. The rugby team and their coach believe that they can win the world Cup for a second time.

4. John's methods are extremely unconventional, like that of Harry, so he did not receive much support from his colleagues.

5. John's methods are extremely unconventional, like those of Harry's, so they did not receive much support from his colleagues.

6. Jerry has tried to climb the mountain several times but so far he has failed to do it.

7. Even though the Board of Trustees agrees with the school principal, they have refused to openly support him.

8. It was shocking to hear the judge address my colleague and me as co-conspirators in the theft.

9. My colleague and me were shocked to hear the judge address us as co-conspirators in the theft.

10. If one wants to do well on the GMAT, you should be willing to work hard and with sustained efforts.

11. When I went back to my hometown for the holidays, I was curious to know what movies they were playing in the theatres.

12. The class consists of more than 200 students, many of who stay in the college dorm itself.

13. The Bermuda Triangle, which is also known as the Devil's Triangle, is a region in the North Atlantic Ocean.

14. The Bermuda Triangle that is also known as the Devil's Triangle is a region in the North Atlantic Ocean.

15. The fashion designer's creations, some of which are very radical, have earned him accolades from the city's style icons.

16. X-rays, which are used to detect bone fractures, are different from those that are used to detect chest infections.

Pronoun Practice Drill – Explanations

1. **Correct Sentence:** Ever since the author criticized his publisher, *the author/the publisher* has been disliked by the masses.

   Explanation: The sentence needs to make it clear who has been disliked by the masses – the author or his publisher.

   ----

2. **Correct Sentence:** The foreign delegation was greeted warmly by the mayor who presented *it* with a report on the development projects underway in the city.

   Explanation: The plural 'them' cannot refer to the singular noun 'delegation'.

   ----

3. **Correct Sentence:** The rugby team and *its* coach believe that they can win the world Cup for a second time.

   Explanation: The singular *team* requires the singular 'its'. The use of 'they' to refer to the team and the coach is correct.

   ----

4. **Correct Sentence:** John's methods are extremely unconventional, like *those* of Harry, so *John* did not receive much support from his colleagues.

   Explanation: The singular 'that' cannot refer to the plural 'methods'. Also 'he' cannot refer to the possessive *John's*.

   ----

5. **Correct Sentence:** John's methods are extremely unconventional, like those of *Harry*, so they did not receive much support from his colleagues.

   Explanation: The possessive *Harry's* is not required because *those* is already referring to the '*methods*'. The use of 'they' to refer to the plural 'methods' is fine – John's colleagues did not support John/John's methods.

   ----

6. **Correct Sentence:** Jerry has tried to climb the mountain several times but so far he has failed to do *so*.

   Explanation: The pronoun 'it' cannot refer to the act of 'failing to climb the mountain'. Use 'so' instead.

   ----

7. **Correct Sentence:** Even though the Board of Trustees agrees with the school principal, *it has* refused to openly support him.

   Explanation: The singular *Board* requires the singular pronoun *it*.

   ----

8. **Correct Sentence:** The sentence is correct as written. In case you are confused, try to read the sentence by omitting 'colleague' from it.

   ----

9. **Correct Sentence:** My colleague and *I* were shocked to hear the judge address us as co-conspirators in the theft

   Explanation: The sentence requires the use of the subjective form 'I'. As in the previous sentence, try reading the sentence by omitting 'colleague' from it.

   ----

10. **Correct Sentence:** If **one wants/you want** to do well on the GMAT, **one/you** should be willing to work hard and with sustained efforts.

    Explanation: *You* and *one* cannot be used interchangeably. Either use 'one' in both the places or use 'you'.

    ----

11. **Correct Sentence:** When I went back to my hometown for the holidays, I was curious to know what movies ***were playing in the theatres/the theatres were playing.***

    Explanation: 'They' does not have any antecedent in the sentence so either 'they' needs to be removed altogether or an antecedent needs to be inserted.

    ----

12. **Correct Sentence:** The class consists of more than 200 students, many of ***whom*** stay in the college dorm itself.

    Explanation: The object form 'whom' is required in the sentence to refer back to the students. In case you are still confused try replacing *who* with *they (subject)/them (object)* and see which one makes sense. *Many of they* makes no sense but *many of them* does; hence, you require the object form of the relative pronoun who i.e. *whom*.

    ----

13. **Correct Sentence:** The sentence is correct as written. 'Which' correctly refers to the Bermuda Triangle.

    ----

14. **Correct Sentence:** The Bermuda Triangle, which is also known as the Devil's Triangle, is a region in the North Atlantic Ocean

    Explanation: In this sentence the use of the restrictive 'that' will be incorrect because this would imply that there are more than one Bermuda Triangles and we are talking about the one that is also known as the Devil's Triangle. However, the part within comma is merely extra information, and so should be introduced by the non restrictive 'which' instead.

    ----

15. **Correct Sentence:** *The creations of the fashion designer*, some of which are very radical, have earned him accolades from the city's leading style icons.

    Explanation: In the original sentence, the objective pronoun *him* cannot refer to the possessive *fashion designer's* so the noun needs to be changed to *'fashion designer'*.

    ----

16. **Correct Sentence:** X-rays *that* are used to detect bone fractures are different from those that are used to detect chest infections.

    Explanation: The sentence compares two different types of x-rays, so we need to use the restrictive 'that' to highlight this difference. The use of 'which' will imply that x-rays are being compared with x-rays. The use of 'those' to refer back to x-rays is correct.

Modification

A Modifier describes and provides a more accurate definitional meaning to another element in a sentence.

For example

John is a good student

In this sentence, *good* is modifying *student*, i.e. it is telling us what type of a student John is.

The two principal modifiers in the English language are **Adjectives** and **Adverbs**. Let's take a look at what they modify:

1. Adjectives modify Nouns & Pronouns

- *Tom Hanks is a **great** actor.* (Adjective *great* modifies the noun *actor*)
- *The drink is in the **tall** glass.* (Adjective *tall* modifies the noun *glass*)

2. Adverbs modify Verbs

- *He walked slowly.* (Adverb *slowly* modifies the verb *walked*)
- *Jake accepted the new task unwillingly.* (Adverb *unwillingly* modifies the verb *accepted*)
- *Michael slept soundly.* (Adverb *soundly* modifies the verb *slept*)

3. Adverbs modify Adjectives

- *They were really happy.* (Adverb *really* modifies the adjective *happy*)
- *My father is completely fearless.* (Adverb *completely* modifies the adjective *fearless*)
- *I know he is very careful.* (Adverb *very* modifies the adjective *careful*)

    (OG 13 – Q 14)
    (OG 12 – Q 12, 40)

In addition, adverbs can also modify other adverbs, clauses, and sentences.

The Proximity Rule for Modification

The modifier should be placed as close as possible to what it modifies.

If the above rule is not followed, the entire meaning of a sentence can change.

For example

- *Only John can eat the pizza*
- *John can only eat the pizza*
- *John can eat the pizza only*

Only is the modifier in the above sentences. Depending on what *only* modifies (John or eat or pizza) the entire meaning of the sentence changes.

Here is another example in which the error looks less obvious (but is definitely there):

The two friends are discussing the soccer match in the stadium.

So where are the two friends? If you've answered *in the stadium* you may not necessarily be correct because it could very well be the match that is in the stadium. In fact the way the sentence is constructed, it is indeed the match that is in the stadium and we don't know where the friends are having their discussion.

If you want to convey the meaning that the two friends are in the stadium, then put the modifying phrase *in the stadium* closer to the two friends:

The two friends are in the stadium discussing the match.

So as a general rule, what is being modified and what is doing the modification – the two should physically be as close to each other as possible.

All that modifiers will test you on is the placement of words, phrases, and clauses in a sentence. This is what makes Modification errors difficult to spot because the sentence may sound and look absolutely correct to you but may still have an error.

How will the GMAT test you on Adjectives & Adverbs?

1) By giving you a choice between an adjective and an adverb

      i.   *My teacher has advised me to do verbal questions regularly.*

     ii.   *My teacher has advised me to do regular verbal questions.*

While the two sentences may look the same, they are in fact conveying very different meanings.

In the first sentence, the adverb *regularly* is modifying the verb *do*. Hence, this sentence means that I should do verbal questions everyday or every other day.

In the second sentence, the adjective *regular* modifies the noun *questions*. Hence, this sentence means that I should do a particular type of verbal questions i.e. the regular ones. I should not do the advanced ones or the easy ones. This sentence does not tell me anything about how regularly I need to do these questions.

Some common adjective-adverb pairs that the GMAT loves to test you on are:

- *Regular/regularly*
- *Economic/economically*
- *Seeming/seemingly*

2) By confusing you with the placement of the adjective/adverb

This comes directly from the proximity rule discussed earlier in this chapter. In this case the sentence will contain either the adjective or the adverb but different options will put the adjective/adverb at different places. You need to identify the correct placement of the same, keeping in mind the overall meaning that the sentence is trying to convey.

- *My dentist **regularly instructs** me to brush my teeth; therefore, I brush my teeth twice a day*
- *My dentist instructs me to **regularly brush** my teeth; therefore, I brush my teeth twice a day.*

As you can see, both of these sentences are grammatically correct but convey different meanings. The first one implies that the dentist instructs me regularly but doesn't tell me anything about how often I should brush my teeth. In contrast, the second one implies that I should brush my teeth regularly but doesn't tell me how often the dentist instructs me.

So then how do we decide which option is correct?

We look at the rest of the sentence. The part after *therefore* states that, as a result of the first part of the sentence, I brush my teeth twice a day i.e. *regularly*. This corresponds to the meaning conveyed by the second sentence, which should be the correct answer.

This is a classic example of a question testing you on the meaning of a sentence. We'll see more of these in the chapter on **Meanings**.

So we've seen how the GMAT is going to test you on adjectives and adverbs. However, the GMAT will not restrict itself to the use of only individual adjectives and adverbs; it will go one step ahead and give you phrases and clauses that again act as adjectives or adverbs – Adjectival phrase/clause and Adverbial phrase/clause.

The Adjectival Phrase/Clause (Noun Modifiers)

These are also known as noun modifiers and function as an adjective i.e. they modify the noun or pronoun in a sentence.

> *John is visiting Japan, the land of the rising sun.*

In this sentence the adjectival phrase *the land of the rising sun* is modifying or describing the noun Japan.

The Touch Rule for Noun Modifiers

In general, a noun modifier (adjectival modifier/participial phrase) must touch the noun or pronoun that it modifies. If we were to rephrase the above example as,

> *John, the land of the rising sun, is visiting Japan.*

This sentence implies that John is the land of the rising sun. This obviously doesn't make any sense.

(OG 13 – Q 22, 35, 82, 87, 110, 135)

However, don't get too carried away by the Touch rule. It is, sometimes, possible for a noun modifier to modify a distant noun as well. For example:

> *The house that is next to the river, dilapidated with age, belongs to my uncle.*

In this sentence the modifying phrase *dilapidated with age* comes next to the river but is obviously referring to the house (the river can't really be dilapidated can it?). In this case the modifying phrase *that is next to the river* is called a vital or essential modifier (because it is vital to identify which house we are talking about) and the phrase *dilapidated with age* is called a non-vital or non-essential modifier (because it gives extra information and the sentence will covey the same meaning even if this were to be removed from the sentence)

(You've seen this earlier in the case of *That vs. Which*)

The major takeaway is that do not follow rules blindly; the sentence eventually has to make sense.

The Adverbial Phrase/Clause

These phrases/clauses can modify the action of the entire preceding clause. They don't have to follow the touch rule and can be used much more freely in a sentence.

> *Michael Phelps won four gold medals in the 2012 summer Olympics, bringing to 18 his overall gold medal count.*

In this sentence the modifying phrase *bringing to 18 his overall gold medal count* is not modifying the closest noun 'Olympics'; rather it is modifying the action of the entire preceding clause and hence is an adverbial modifier.

(OG 13 – Q 111)

(OG 12 – Q 47, 94)

Do not get too bogged down by Noun and Adverbial modifiers. The GMAT will test you on these in limited ways, which we will discuss now. As long you are aware of (and look out for) these, you will not face any problems tackling Modification questions on the GMAT.

How will Modifications be tested on the GMAT?

The GMAT generally deals with modifying phrases. Usually set off by commas, modifying phrases provide more information about the subject or object in the main clause of the sentence without naming it directly. In order for a modifying phrase to be used correctly, it must be placed as close as possible to the object or person that it modifies. The following are some typical ways in which the GMAT can test you on these:

1) Misplaced Modifiers

In an effort to do well in the exam, ten hours of study were put in everyday by John.

The phrase **In an effort to do well on the exam** is called a modifying phrase because it is modifying a subject (which is not contained within the phrase). The person who is making the effort is the subject of the sentence i.e. *John*.

Per the Proximity rule mentioned earlier, the modifier must be as close as possible to what it modifies, but in the above sentence the modifying phrase is followed by *ten hours*.

Hence, this is a case of a misplaced modifier; the correct sentence should have the subject i.e. *John*, immediately after the comma.

In an effort to do well in the exam, John put in ten hours of study every day.

It is usually quite easy to identify misplaced modifiers – whenever a sentence begins with a modifying phrase (especially one that starts with an *-ing* word) followed by a comma, the noun or pronoun following the comma should be what the phrase is referring to.

However, do not assume that a modifying phrase can come only at the beginning of a sentence; it can come in the middle or even at the end.

Modifying phrase in the middle,

John, a laptop mechanic, came to my house yesterday. (modifying phrase **a laptop mechanic** is modifying the subject **John**)

You cannot say - John came to my house yesterday, a laptop mechanic.

(OG 13 – Q 22)

Modifying phrase at the end,

Jack is travelling to Japan, the land of the rising sun. (modifying phrase **the land of the rising sun** is modifying **Japan**)

Here are two common forms of Misplaced Modifiers on the GMAT

i) **Participial Phrase** – A phrase that starts with a present or a past participle (may or may not be preceded by a preposition). Whenever a sentence starts with a participial phrase there will almost always be a misplaced modifier lurking around the corner.

Examples

Incorrect: *Educated at Eton and then at Oxford, it was surprising that George could not get into a decent business school.* (Sentence starts with the past participle *educated*, the one who was educated i.e. *George* should come after the comma and not *it*)

Correct: *Educated at Eton and then at Oxford, George surprisingly could not get into a decent business school.*

(OG 13 – Q 62, 65, 68)

ii) **Adjectives or Adjectival Phrase**

Examples,

Incorrect: *Tall and handsome, a striking figure was cut by John.*

Correct: *Tall and handsome, John cut a striking figure.*

An adjectival phrase is a group of words that acts as an adjective by modifying a noun

Incorrect: *Known for its strong sense of ethics, one of India's most respected conglomerates is the Tata group.*

Correct: *Known for its strong sense of ethics, the Tata group is one of India's most respected conglomerates.*

2) Dangling Modifiers & Introducing new words

Usually, it is suggested that you do not add additional words to the original sentence, but sometimes you may have to add in new words to make the meaning of the sentence clear, especially on Modification questions.

For example

Using a stethoscope, heartbeats can be detected.

This sentence sounds fine but, using the knowledge of Modification that you have acquired in this chapter, you know that this cannot be correct, since what follows the comma should be the person who is using the stethoscope. Since no such person is mentioned in the original sentence, the modifying phrase *Using a stethoscope* is called a dangling modifier.

To correct this error, you will have to add in a new word to the sentence to make it correct, such as

Using a stethoscope, a doctor can detect heartbeats

Author's Tip – *Whenever a sentence starts with an -ing word (technically called a participial phrase), it will almost always be a modification question with the noun that is doing the action of the -ing word coming immediately after the comma.*

For example

- *Rivaling the Taj Mahal in beauty,......* (whatever is rivaling the Taj should come after the comma)

- *Running the first mile quickly,.......* (whoever is running the first mile quickly should come after the comma)

- *Looking fitter than ever, ...*(whoever is looking fitter than ever should come after the comma)

(OG 13 – Q 74)

3) Watch out for the Possessive trap

When a modifying phrase is followed by a possessive noun, double check whether the phrase is modifying the correct subject.

Incorrect: *Coming out of the house, John's laptop was stolen.*

Even though this sentence may sound correct, it is actually incorrect because the subject is *John's laptop* and not *John*. So, the modifying phrase *Coming out of the house* is incorrectly modifying *John's laptop* in the original sentence making it appear as though John's laptop was coming out of the house.

Correct: *Coming out of the house, John was robbed of his laptop.*

(OG 13 – Q 19, 59, 68, 135)
(OG 12 – Q 58, 135)

4) Back to back Modifying Phrases

Consider the following sentence:

The fifth student in the row, next to the girl with braids, wearing a red shirt, is my son.

In this sentence you are using two back to back modifying phrases – *next to the girl with braids and wearing a red shirt* – leading to lots of confusion! Is the girl wearing the red shirt or is the son wearing it? To avoid such confusion, it is always incorrect to use two back to back modifying phrases.

This will of course only be the case when both the phrases are essential or non essential. If one phrase is essential and the other non essential, then the sentence is correct. For example in the sentence we saw earlier - *The house that is next to the river, dilapidated with age, belongs to my uncle* – an essential and a non essential modifier are used back to back. There is nothing wrong with this sentence.

(OG 13 – Q 104, 106)

Exceptions to the Modification Rule

While in general a modifying phrase must be placed immediately next to the subject that it is intended to modify, there may be certain cases in which this rule can be relaxed a little. These will almost always involve the use of relative pronouns such as 'that', and 'who'.

i) *Terry has a penthouse in the city's tallest building that he uses to entertain his clients.* (**That** obviously refers to the penthouse and not to the building)

ii) *A President has finally been elected who will try to reverse the tide of unemployment and poverty in the country.*

Modifiers Practice Drill

Identify the errors of Modification in each the following sentences and try to come up with the correct answer. Some sentences may have more than one correct answer and some may be correct as written.

1. Trevor and McCormick are discussing the butterfly in the garden. (The butterfly is in their books).

2. Having topped his class throughout school, Tim's grades did not surprise anyone.

3. Using a guitar, music can be created.

4. Richard won the boxing match easily, sinewy and strong.

5. While they did not work last year, analysts believe that the company's strategies may just bear fruit this year.

6. The accused said in his home he had all the required proof

7. Not something Tim was known for, he surprised everyone with his perceptiveness

8. Sharing its borders with France and Germany, Switzerland's watches and chocolates are famous all over the world.

9. Having spent most of his time in tropical countries, John found the Russian weather unbearable cold

10. Having learnt acting from the best in the business, tall and handsome, the actor looks set to become a superstar

11. To ensure that a product sells well, it has to be introduced gradually to the market

12. Gotham city witnessed yet another shooting incident just two days after a robbery and firing took place outside the city park, this time in the Northern suburbs.

13. Noticing a large police contingent on the road, the assailant panicked and, leaving his weapons behind, abandoning the car and escaping

14. Shedding his usual reticence, the President of the citizen's group spearheaded a sharp attack on the city Municipal Commissioner, forced the Commissioner to unconditionally withdraw his

disparaging reference to the economically backward citizens of the city

15. California has been a natural choice of most consulting companies, being home to head offices or delivery centres of some of the world's biggest companies.

16. The brainchild of two college dropouts now settled in London, a team of healthcare and technology professionals formally founded Meditech.

17. Stating the desire of most students to pursue management education abroad as a trend that is expected to grow manifold over the next few years, the company's intentions of making huge capital expenditures are justified

18. A person's appearance can be ruined by poor cared for shoes

19. Until recently, the seeming/seemingly conflict of interest wouldn't have mattered much to John but now it does.

20. The car in front of me was moving so slow that I had to overtake it from the wrong side.

Modifiers Practice Drill – Explanations

1. **Correct Answer:** Trevor and McCormick are in the garden discussing the butterfly.

   Explanation: Since the prepositional phrase 'in the garden' refers to Trevor and McCormick and not to the butterfly, this phrase should be placed closer to Trevor and McCormick.

   ----

2. **Correct Answer:** Having topped his class throughout school, Tim did not surprise anyone when he scored good grades.

   Explanation: The modifying phrase *'Having topped his class throughout school'* incorrectly modifies *Tim's grades*. The phrase should actually modify *Tim*.

   ----

3. **Correct Answer:** Using a guitar, a musician can create music.

   Explanation: The sentence starts with the modifying phrase *'Using a guitar'*, so whoever is using the guitar needs to come immediately after the comma. In this case, since the sentence has no subject, we'll have to add one – the musician.

   ----

4. **Correct Answer:** Richard, sinewy and strong, won the boxing match easily.

   Explanation: The adjectival phrase *sinewy and strong* is modifying the noun *Richard* and hence should touch *Richard*.

   ----

5. **Correct Answer:** While they did not work last year, the company's strategies, analysts believe, may just bear fruit this year.

   Explanation: The sentence starts with a modifying phrase *While they did not work last year*, so whatever did not work earlier needs to come after this phrase – the *company's strategies* and not *the analysts*.

   ----

6. **Correct Answer:** The accused said that in his home he had all the required proof.

            OR

            The accused said in his home that he had all the required proof.

   Explanation: The original sentence can be interpreted in two ways as written above. The usage of 'that' in the correct place will specify which of the two meanings the sentence is trying to convey.

   ----

7. **Correct Answer:** Not something Tim was known for, his perceptiveness surprised everyone.

    Explanation: The modifying phrase *Not something Tim was known for* refers to *Tim's perceptiveness* and not to *Tim*.

    ----

8. **Correct Answer:** Sharing its borders with France and Germany, Switzerland is famous all over the world for its chocolates and watches.

    Explanation: The modifying phrase *Sharing its borders with France and Germany* refers to *Switzerland* and not to its watches and chocolates.

    ----

9. **Correct Answer:** Having spent most of his time in tropical countries, John found the Russian weather unbearably cold.

    Explanation: We require the adverb *unbearably* to modify the adjective *cold*. (*cold* is modifying the noun *weather*)

    ----

10. **Correct Answer:** Having learnt acting from the best in the business, the actor, tall and handsome, looks set to become a superstar.

    Explanation: The sentence starts with two back to back modifying phrases. Placing the subject *the actor* in between the two corrects this error.

    ----

11. **Correct Answer:** To ensure that a product sells well, its manufacturer has to gradually introduce it to the market.

    Explanation: The sentence starts with a modifying phrase *To ensure that a product sells well*. Someone needs to be doing this ensuring, so we will have to insert a subject after the comma – *its manufacturer, a company, a CEO, etc.*

    ----

12. **Correct Answer:** Gotham city witnessed yet another shooting incident, this time in the Northern suburbs, just two days after a robbery and firing took place outside the city park.

    Explanation: The modifying phrase *this time in the Northern suburbs* obviously refers to the current shooting incident and hence needs to be placed next to it in the sentence.

    ----

13. **Correct Answer:** Noticing a large police contingent on the road, the assailant panicked and, leaving his weapons behind, abandoned the car and escaped.

Explanation: This is a mix of a modification and a parallel structure question. In its current form, the sentence doesn't make much sense because it ends with two back to back modifying phrases. To correct this, change the participles in the last part of the sentence to verbs – abandoned and escaped.

---

14. **Correct Answer:** Shedding his usual reticence, the President of the citizens group spearheaded a sharp attack on the city Municipal Commissioner, forcing the Commissioner to unconditionally withdraw his disparaging reference to the economically backward citizens of the city.

    Explanation: The sentence as written is incorrect. If you are trying to say that the President of the citizens group did two things – spearheaded and forced – then you need an 'and' before 'forced' but the sentence doesn't have this.

    In fact the President of the citizens group just did one thing – spearhead a sharp attack. As a result of this attack the Municipal Commissioner had to withdraw his disparaging remarks. So it's best if we use the participle 'forcing' thereby converting that entire clause into an adverbial modifier modifying the action of the entire previous clause.

---

15. **Correct Answer:** California, home to head offices or delivery centres of some of the world's biggest companies, has been a natural choice of most consulting companies.

    Explanation: The modifying phrase *home to head offices or delivery centres of some of the world's biggest companies* needs to be next to California and not to consulting companies.

---

16. **Correct Answer:** The brainchild of two college dropouts now settled in London, Meditech was formally founded by a team of healthcare and technology professionals.

    Explanation: The sentence starts with a modifying phrase *The brainchild of two college dropouts now settled in London,* so what was this brainchild needs to follow the comma – obviously Meditech.

---

17. **Correct Answer:** Stating the desire of most students to pursue management education abroad as a trend that is expected to grow manifold over the next few years, the company justified its intentions of making huge capital expenditures.

    Explanation: The sentence starts with a modifying phrase *stating the desire..........few years,* so whoever is stating this desire needs to come after the comma – the company and not its intentions.

---

18. **Correct Answer:** A person's appearance can be ruined by poorly cared for shoes.

    Explanation: You require the adverb *poorly* to modify the adjective *cared*.

----

19. **Correct Answer:** Until recently, the seeming conflict of interest wouldn't have mattered much to John but now it does.

    Explanation: You require the adjective *seeming* to modify the noun phrase *conflict of interest*.

----

20. **Correct Answer:** The car in front of me was moving so slowly that I had to overtake it from the wrong side.

    Explanation: You require the adverb *slowly* to modify the verb *moving*.

Parallel Structure

Parallel Structure or Parallelism is one error type in which you can get from the easiest to the most difficult of questions. It's not surprising that this is the most common error type tested in the OGs.

Looking at it conceptually, parallel structure is all about consistency. Whenever you come across a sentence that contains a list or series of items or actions (typically separated by commas), you should immediately know that you have come across a Parallel Structure question.

For example

Jerry likes walking and to swim.

In this sentence the gerund *walking* is not parallel to the infinitive *to swim*. The correct sentence will read,

Jerry likes walking and swimming.

OR

Jerry likes to walk and to swim.

Now let's look at another sentence,

- *Tom can go to his school by bus, train, or cab.*
- *Tom can go to his school by bus, train, or by cab.*
- *Tom can go to his school by bus, by train, or by cab.*

The first option is correct, since it is implied that 'by' applies to the other two options as well; the third option is also correct for the same reason (albeit wordy); however, the second option is incorrect because it implies that 'by' is needed only for the bus and the cab and that 'by' is not needed for the train. So, as stated earlier, consistency is the key to identifying and answering parallelism questions.

1. **Parallel Structure with Nouns**

    - She bought a *skirt* and a *blouse*.

2. **Parallel Structure with Adjectives**

    - The canoes are *light* but *sturdy*.

3. **Parallel Structure with Adverbs**

    - The tiger walked *slowly* and *menacingly* towards its prey.

4. Parallel Structure with Verbs

When you have more than one verb in a sentence, be sure to make the verbs parallel by not shifting tenses unnecessarily. Also, don't shift from an active to a passive verb.

- **Correct** - John *prepared* the presentation on the train and *delivered* it at the meeting. *(parallel: both verbs are active and in the simple past tense)*
- **Incorrect** - John *prepared* the presentation on the plane, and it *was delivered* by him at the meeting. *(faulty parallelism: active and passive verb)*

(OG 13 – Q 64, 114)

5. Parallel Structure with Infinitives

- **Correct** - Jessica likes *to sing, to dance,* and *to play* the cello.
- **Correct** - Jessica likes *to sing, dance,* and *play* the cello.
- **Incorrect** - Jessica likes *to sing, to dance,* and *play* the cello.

(OG 13 – Q 18, 55)

6. Parallel Structure with Gerunds

- **Correct** - John likes *hiking, swimming,* and *cycling.*
- **Incorrect** - John likes *hiking, swimming,* and *to ride* a bicycle.

(OG 12 – Q 119)

7. Parallel Structure with Clauses

- **Incorrect** - The teacher suggested *that the students come* to class on time and *complete* their homework assignments regularly.
- **Correct** - The teacher suggested *that the students come* to class on time and *that they complete* their homework assignments regularly.

8. Parallel Structure with Correlative conjunctions

Correlative conjunctions, in simple English, are pairs of words that always go together. If you have the first word present in a sentence, the second has to be there as well, else the sentence is considered incorrect.

Examples
- *Not only…..but also*
- *No sooner….than*
- *Either … or*
- *Neither … nor*
- *Both … and*

Important - Correlative conjunctions always join grammatically equal elements (e.g., noun & noun, adjective & adjective, phrase & phrase, clause & clause, etc.). They also lend equal weight to the joined elements i.e. one joined element is always equal to but never subordinate to the other.

Correct: The workers disputed <u>not only</u> *the magazine article* <u>but also</u> *the company's official statement.* (parallel: phrase with phrase)

Incorrect: The workers disputed <u>not only</u> *the magazine article* <u>but also</u> *they disputed the company's official statement.* (faulty parallelism: phrase with clause)

Correct: <u>Either</u> *I like the job* <u>or</u> *I don't like it.* (parallel: clause matched with clause)

Correct: <u>Either</u> *I like the job* <u>or</u> *I don't.* (parallel: clause matched with clause)

Incorrect: <u>Either</u> *I like the job* <u>or</u> *not.* (faulty parallelism: clause matched with adverb)

Correct: I have <u>neither</u> *the patience* <u>nor</u> *the desire* to complete the assignment. (parallel: noun phrase with noun phrase)

Incorrect: I have <u>neither</u> *the patience* <u>nor</u> *do I desire* to complete the assignment. (faulty parallelism: phrase matched with clause)

Important: When using correlative conjunctions, the construction that comes after the first conjunction must be repeated after the second.

Correct: *John is neither from Paris nor from Germany.*

Incorrect: *John is neither from Paris nor Germany*

Since *from* comes after *neither*, it needs to be repeated after *nor* as well; else the sentence will be incorrect. However, if *from* were to come before *neither*, then it does not need to be repeated after *nor* because it is assumed that *from* applies to both *neither and nor*; repeating *from* in this case would actually be incorrect.

Correct: *John is from neither Paris nor Germany.*

Incorrect: *John is from neither Paris nor from Germany*

(OG 13 – Q 15, 56, 57, 84, 86, 109)
(OG 12 – Q 56, 81, 96, 109)

What to make Parallel – Check for Meaning

It is important that you use common sense while deciding which parts of a sentence to make parallel. Consider the following sentence:

> *The fare from London to New York is $880 including airfare from London, spending two days at the Grand Hotel, and taking a trip to Liberty Island.*

If you look at this sentence with a myopic vision (i.e. without understanding its meaning) you might think it gets the parallel construction right – **including, spending, and taking, all end with** *-ing.*

However, if you read the sentence again, you'll realize that *including* is common to all three things so what actually has to be made parallel are the nouns airfare, two days at the Grand Hotel, and a trip to Liberty Island.

So the correct sentence should read:

> *The fare from London to New York is $880 including airfare from London, two days at the Grand Hotel, and a trip to Liberty Island.*

How about this one then,

> *After the typhoon, the citizens of the county were left without food, power, and huge bills for reconstructing their houses.*

When a preposition such as *without* is used in front of only the first member of a series, it's taken to refer to all the members of the series. In the context of this sentence, this means that the citizens were left without food, without power, and without huge bills for reconstructing their houses. The last part obviously doesn't make sense and can be corrected by rewriting the sentence.

Correct: *After the typhoon, the citizens of the county were left without food, without power, and with huge bills for reconstructing their houses.*

Correct: *After the typhoon, the citizens of the county were left without food and power, and with huge bills for reconstructing their houses.*

So to summarize, make it a point to understand the meaning of a sentence before you decide what aspects to make parallel. Making things parallel blindly could land you in trouble, especially on high difficulty questions.

(OG 13 – Q 112, 134)

Parallelism with Gerund Phrases and Action Nouns

Before getting into parallelism rules for gerund phrases and action nouns, let's understand what these terms actually mean.

Gerund Phrase

We saw in the earlier section that gerunds are verbs that act as nouns. A Gerund Phrase is a group of words that starts with a gerund and will include other modifiers or objects. For example,

- *Exercising daily* is good for the health.

- *Running very quickly* can be bad for your knees.

As you can see, in both these sentences the gerund phrase is the subject of the verb. This is what separates a gerund phrase from participial phrases. A participial phrase will always modify the subject of the sentence but it will never be the subject itself. For example,

- *Running very quickly,* Usain Bolt won the race.

In this sentence the phrase *Running very quickly* is acting as an adjective to modify the subject *Usain Bolt*. You've already seen these phrases in the previous chapter on Modifiers.

The examples above are all *Simple Gerund Phrases* i.e. phrases that start with a gerund and contain other modifiers and objects.

There is also something called a **Complex Gerund Phrase**, which almost always starts with an article (a, an, or the) and includes a preposition after the gerund. For example,

- *Selling books* is a good business (Simple gerund phrase)

- *The selling of books* is a good business (Complex gerund phrase)

Action Nouns

Action nouns are obviously action words that are used as nouns in a sentence. So what is the difference between Action nouns and Gerunds?

The following sentences should make this clear:

- The *inspection* of records is a tedious process. (Action noun)

- *Inspecting records* is a tedious process. (Simple Gerund Phrase)

- *The inspecting of records* is a tedious process (Complex Gerund Phrase)

So gerunds will always include the *-ing* form of the verb whereas action nouns will not.

Parallelism Rules for Gerund Phrases & Action Nouns

Now that you know what are Simple Gerund Phrases, Complex Gerund Phrases, and Action Nouns, here are the parallelism rules to follow when the sentence includes any/all of these:

i) **A Simple Gerund Phrase can never be parallel to a Complex Gerund Phrase or to an Action Noun.**

Incorrect: *Selling books* is a better business than *the selling of coffee*. (Simple gerund phrase and complex gerund phrase)

Correct: *Selling books* is a better business than *selling coffee*. (Both simple gerund phrases)

Correct: *The selling of books* is a better business than *the selling of coffee*. (Both complex gerund phrases)

ii) **A Complex Gerund Phrase can be parallel to another Complex Gerund Phrase and also to Action Nouns**

Correct: *The raising of* the white flag and the *release* of prisoners are signs of peace. (Complex gerund phrase and action noun)

Correct: The raising of the white flag is as important as the lowering of weapons. (Both complex gerund phrases)

iii) **Always prefer Action Nouns to Complex Gerund Phrases**

If an action noun exists for a verb, then prefer it to the complex gerund phrase.

Incorrect: *The raising of* the white flag and *the releasing of* prisoners are signs of peace.

The releasing of prisoners is a complex gerund phrase but there is already an action noun in the English language that denotes the same – release. So prefer *release* to the use of the complex gerund phrase.

Correct: *The raising of* the white flag and *the release of* prisoners are signs of peace. (Complex gerund phrase and action noun)

(OG 13 – Q 121)
(OG 12 – Q 28, 119, 130)

Parallelism with Past and Present Participles:

- *The students, tired after the test and wanting to reach home quickly, took a short cut.*

- *The students, tired after the test and wanted to reach home quickly, took a short cut.*

- *The students, tiring after the test and wanting to reach home quickly, took a short cut.*

If you were to get the above choices in a question and if you were in a hurry, you would most likely go with options two or three because *tired* and *wanted* look parallel and so do *tiring* and *wanting*.

However if you concentrate a little, you will notice that both these choices seem or sound incorrect, and rightly so. In fact option one is the correct sentence.

This is because *tired* and *wanting* are both used as adjectives (the past and the present participles, respectively), and hence correctly modify the noun *students*.

Option two uses *wanted* as a verb, which obviously can't parallel the adjective *tired*. Similarly option three also distorts the meaning by suggesting that the students are *tiring* after the test whereas the students are already *tired*.

So the takeaway for you is that a past participle can be parallel to a present participle because they are both in essence adjectives.

(OG 12 – Q 42)

The use of *that* twice in a sentence:

> *My trainer suggests **that**, in order to lose weight quickly, I cut out all carbohydrates from my diet and **that** I exercise for at least an hour every day.*

The reason this sentence uses *that* twice is because the trainer is actually making two suggestions – one about the diet and one about the exercise – so *that* needs to be repeated before each suggestion to maintain parallelism.

If you don't repeat the *that*, then you are implying that the trainer has actually made only one suggestion. So it will again come down to your understanding of the meaning of the sentence correctly.

(OG 13 – Q 47, 128)
(OG 12 – Q 48, 128, 139)

Important Parallelism Markers:

To make it easier to identify Parallelism errors, look out for the following common parallelism markers. If you spot any of these in a sentence, immediately check the sentence for parallelism.

- *And*
- *Or*
- *Either…..or*
- *Neither….nor*
- *Not only/just…..but also*
- *Both…….and*

Parallelism Practice Drill

Check each of the following sentences for the error of faulty Parallelism and come up with the correct sentence. Some sentences may be correct as written.

1. John did not like his new workplace because he could not leave early, come late, and he could not take long lunch breaks

2. His remarks suggested both sarcasm as well as bitterness

3. To become successful in life, one not only has to be willing to work hard but also he has to have some luck on his side

4. The CEO has decided to reduce costs, staff strength, and increase revenues

5. Modern cars are constructed either from aluminium or carbon fibre

6. The selling of books is a better business than selling grocery

7. Business expenditure, including the expenditure on entertaining clients, is different from spending on one's own entertainment

8. Performance consultancies help in identifying high potential leaders, creating a leadership pipeline, building engagement, more efficient hiring processes, and rewarding employees for good performance

9. A few of the crimes that hit headlines in the last few months, including the murder of a senior citizen, the looting of a bank ATM, and cloned credit cards, is/are yet to be cracked.

10. The CEO said that as markets grow and with the intensification of competition, companies will have to come up with more and more innovative strategies to acquire customers.

11. A typical intervention can have several customer interaction points such as training workshops, coaching, on the job training, and lasting from four to six months

12. While selecting a perfume, experts suggest that you select a scent that complements your personality and that it works with your skin.

13. Olfactory experts suggest that, while selecting a perfume, you select not only a scent that complements your personality but also one that works with your skin.

14. Kramer realizes that he will have to explain to the re-settlers how they are going to eat, access water, and about energy use

Parallelism Practice Drill – Explanations

1. **Correct Answer:** John did not like his new workplace because he could not leave early, come late, and take long lunch breaks.

   Explanation: The three items at the end of the sentence - leave early, come late, and he could not take long lunch breaks – need to be parallel.

   ----

2. **Correct Answer:** His remarks suggested both sarcasm and bitterness.

           OR

           His remarks suggested sarcasm as well as bitterness.

   Explanation: The correct idiom is 'both X **and** Y'. Or, if you wish to use 'as well as', then remove 'both' from the sentence.

   ----

3. **Correct Answer:** To become successful in life, one not only has to be willing to work hard but also has to have some luck on his side.

   Explanation: What comes after *not only* needs to be repeated after *but also*. Since 'one' is before *not only*, 'one/he' does not need to be repeated after *but also*.

   ----

4. **Correct Answer:** The CEO has decided to reduce costs and staff strength and increase revenues.

   Explanation: While the sentence may look correct as written it has an error of meaning. The CEO has decided to reduce two things – costs and staff strength – and increase one thing – revenues. Thus, there needs to be an extra *and* between the two things that he has decided to reduce.

   ----

5. **Correct Answer:** Modern cars are constructed either from aluminium or from carbon fibre.

   Explanation: Since *from* comes after *either*, it need to be repeated after *or*.

   ----

6. **Correct Answer:** Selling books is a better business than selling grocery.

           OR

           The selling of books is a better business than the selling of grocery.

   Explanation: The sentence compares a simple gerund phrase with a complex gerund phrase. To maintain parallelism put a simple/complex gerund phrase on both sides

   ----

7. **Correct Answer:** Business expenditure, including the expenditure on entertaining clients, is different from personal expenditure.

    Explanation: The noun phrase 'business expenditure' is not parallel to the gerund + prepositional phrase combination *'spending on one's own entertainment'*, so change this to a noun phrase as well.

    ----

8. **Correct Answer:** Performance consultancies help in identifying high potential leaders, creating a leadership pipeline, building engagement, making hiring processes more efficient, and rewarding employees for good performance.

    Explanation: According to the sentence, performance consultancies help in doing five things. Four of these things start with participles – identifying, creating, building, and rewarding – so the fifth also needs to start with a participle i.e. *making*.

    ----

9. **Correct Answer:** A few of the crimes that hit headlines in the last few months, including the murder of a senior citizen, the looting of a bank ATM, and the cloning of credit cards, is/**are** yet to be cracked.

    Explanation: The first two crimes are in the form of an action noun and a complex gerund phrase, so the third crime should also be a complex gerund phrase. The correct verb should be the plural *are* to match the subject *crimes*.

    ----

10. **Correct Answer:** The CEO said that as markets grow and as competition intensifies, companies will have to come up with more and more innovative strategies to acquire customers.

    Explanation: The two things that the CEO said need to be parallel, so they both need to start with '*as*'.

    ----

11. **Correct Answer:** A typical intervention can have several customer interaction points such as training workshops, coaching, and on the job training, and can last from four to six months.

    Explanation: The sentence tells us two things about a typical intervention – that it can have several customer interaction points and that it can last from four to six months. Obviously these two need to be parallel. Again there's a sub list of three things within the customer interaction points; we need to use an *and* before the last item in this sub list.

    ----

12. **Correct Answer:** While selecting a perfume, experts suggest that you select a scent that complements your personality and that works with your skin.

Explanation: According to the sentence, the chosen scent should do two things – complement your personality and work with your skin. Both these things come after the relative pronoun *that*. Since *scent* comes before *that*, it is assumed that it applies to both the relative clauses starting with *that*; hence, we don't need to repeat the 'it' (to refer back to scent) in the second clause.

----

13. **Correct Answer:** The sentence is correct as written. Since *scent* comes after *not only*, it needs to be repeated after *but also*; hence the use of *one* to refer back to *scent* is correct.

----

14. **Correct Answer:** Kramer realizes that he will have to explain to the re-settlers how they are going to eat, access water, and use energy.

Explanation: The phrase *going to* applies to all the three things at the end of the sentence – eat, access water, and use energy. The use of *about* before the last item in this list makes no sense, so remove it.

Comparison

Comparison questions are a special category of Parallel Structure questions that involve two or more items being compared with one another.

Compared Items must be Logically similar

In simple language, while comparing two things, compare apples with apples and oranges with oranges.

> *The students in my class are smarter than other classes.*

This sentence is incorrect because it compares *students* with *classes*. The correct sentence should read,

> *The students in my class are smarter than the students in other classes.*
>
> *OR*
>
> *The students in my class are smarter than those in other classes.*

(OG 13 – Q 9, 11, 20, 24, 31, 43, 98, 124, 136, 139)

Compared Items must be Grammatically similar

This is the same as with Parallel Construction questions – compare nouns with nouns, verbs with verbs, and so on. Do NOT compare a noun with a verb or an adjective with an adverb, etc.

> *I enjoy reading novels more than to watch movies.* (compares participle *reading* with infinitive *to watch*, so not parallel)

The correct sentence should read,

> *I enjoy reading novels more than watching movies.*

How will Comparisons be tested on the GMAT

1) Unclear Comparisons

Incorrect: *John loves Tina more than Katy.*

This sentence can be interpreted in two ways – either John loves Tina more than he loves Katy or John loves Tina more than Katy loves Tina. The problem can be corrected by adding some more words to the sentence.

Correct: *John loves Tina more than he does Katy*

Correct: *John loves Tina more than Katy does*

2) Illogical Comparisons

Incorrect: *The books at this shop are much more interesting than any other shop.*

This sentence quite absurdly compares books with other shops, which obviously does not make any sense.

Correct: *The books at this shop are much more interesting than the books at any other shop.*

Correct: *The books at this shop are much more interesting than those at any other shop.*

3) The use of Comparative and Superlative forms

When comparing two things, use the comparative form *(more/er)*, and when comparing more than two things, use the superlative form *(most/est)*.

Incorrect: *Among all my students, John is **more** intelligent.*

Correct: *Among all my students, John is the **most** intelligent.*

Incorrect: *Between the two of them, his idea is the **best***

Correct: *Between the two of them, his idea is **better***

Also remember that if a sentence starts with a comparative such as *the more, the higher, etc.,* the second clause of the sentence will also start with a comparative.

For example:

Incorrect: *The more John studies, he will score even higher.*

Correct: *The more John studies, the higher he will score.*

(OG 13 – Q 2)

4) The use of *Like* and *As*

A common problem faced by most students is when to use *Like* and when to use *As*.

Since *Like* is a preposition and *As* is a conjunction, use *like* only to compare nouns and *as* for all other comparisons (e.g. while comparing clauses)

Examples:

1. *John & Jacob, as/**like** their father Mark, are excellent players of chess.*

   In this sentence, John & Jacob are nouns that are being compared with another noun Mark. Hence, the correct word here is 'like'.

2. *Just **as**/like reading is good for the mind, running is good for the body.*

   In this sentence, two clauses 'reading is good for the mind' and 'running is good for the body' are being compared, so the correct word is 'as'.

   (OG 13 – Q 11, 85)
   (OG 12 – Q 65, 82)

Author's Tip – Whenever you spot the following words in a sentence - *like, unlike, than, as many, as much* - check for Comparison error.

Comparison Practice Drill

Check each of the following sentences for the error of illogical comparison and come up with the correct sentence. Some sentences may be correct as written.

1. He must be treated like/as any ordinary citizen.

2. He must be treated like/as any ordinary citizen would be in a similar situation.

3. Common sense would suggest that the management could have done much more to prevent the talks from collapsing as/than it did.

4. The NYPD believes that it has controlled crime better this year than 2011.

5. As/Like the University of Pennsylvania, several other higher education institutes like Boston University and the University of North Carolina are increasing their focus on global leadership programs

6. John's shirt, like that of his brother's, is pink in colour

7. Like many politicians, the senator's promises sounded great but ultimately led to nothing.

8. Marine zoologists maintain that porpoises have powers of attention more sustained than that of chimpanzees

9. The cost of a year at college these days is greater than a house.

10. Charlie's assumption, unlike James', was that the customers would attend the workshop just because the head of business was conducting it.

11. Between the two movies, one from the horror genre and one from the comedy genre, the horror one is best.

12. Of the numerous decisions facing the Supreme Court this term, the question of an individual's right to die is certainly the more perplexing.

Comparison Practice Drill – Explanations

1.   **Correct Answer:** He must be treated **like**/as any ordinary citizen.

     Explanation: You use *like* to compare two nouns – he and any ordinary citizen.

     ----

2.   **Correct Answer:** He must be treated like/**as** any ordinary citizen would be in a similar situation

     Explanation: In this sentence you are comparing two clauses – how he would be treated vis a vis how any ordinary citizen would be treated. Hence, go with *as*.

     ----

3.   **Correct Answer:** Common sense would suggest that the management could have done much more to prevent the talks from collapsing as/**than** it did.

     Explanation: The correct idiom is *more....than* and not *more....as*.

     ----

4.   **Correct Answer:** The NYPD believes that it has controlled crime better this year than it did in 2011.

     Explanation: The original sentence incorrectly compares the clause *how NYPD has controlled crime this year* with the noun *2011*. The correct comparison will have another clause after *than* as well.

     ----

5.   **Correct Answer:** As/**Like** the University of Pennsylvania, several other higher education institutes ~~like~~ **such as** Boston University and the University of North Carolina are increasing their focus on global leadership programs.

     Explanation: Use *like* to compare the nouns – universities. Also use *such as* (and not *like*) to give examples.

     ----

6.   **Correct Answer:** John's shirt, like that of his brother, is pink in colour.
                         OR
                         John's shirt, like his brother's, is pink in colour.

Explanation: The original sentence compares John's shirt with something (that) of his brother's shirt; this is obviously incorrect because the idea is to compare the two shirts. So, either use the possessive *brother's* or use the pronoun *that*, but not both.

----

7. **Correct Answer:** Like those of many politicians, the senator's promises sounded great but ultimately led to nothing.

   Explanation: The original sentence incorrectly compares many politicians with the senator's promises. We can correct this by adding a 'those' to the first part to refer to promises.

----

8. **Correct Answer:** Marine zoologists maintain that porpoises have powers of attention more sustained than those of chimpanzees.

   Explanation: The original sentence incorrectly uses the singular 'that' to refer to the *powers of attention* of chimpanzees; we need the plural *those* instead.

----

9. **Correct Answer:** The cost of a year at college these days is greater than **the cost/that** of a house.

   Explanation: The original sentence incorrectly compares *cost of a year at college* to *a house* and not to the *cost of a house*.

----

10. **Correct Answer: The sentence is correct as written**. It correctly compares Charlie's assumption with James' assumption. Remember that the possessive form of a name ending with 's' (such as James) only takes an apostrophe at the end without the 's'.

----

11. **Correct Answer:** Between the two movies, one from the horror genre and one from the comedy genre, the horror one is **better**.

   Explanation: When comparing two things, use the comparative form *better* and not the superlative form *best*.

----

12. **Correct Answer:** Of the numerous decisions facing the Supreme Court this term, the question of an individual's right to die is certainly the **most** perplexing.

   Explanation: When comparing more than two things (numerous decisions), use the superlative form *most* and not the comparative form *more*.

Idioms
&
Style

Idioms are probably the trickiest aspect of Sentence Correction questions, primarily because we use a lot of them incorrectly in our day to day English usage.

For example,

A) John has **forbidden** his daughter **from** going out in the night.

B) The GMAT **comprises of** AWA, IR, Quant, and Verbal sections.

C) The President of the United States is **considered to be** the most powerful person in the world.

D) I **believe** John's version **as the truth**.

As some of you must have already spotted, all of these sentences are incorrect.

A – the correct idiom is *forbidden to* & not *forbidden from*

B – *comprises* does not take an *of*

C – *considered* does not take *to be*

D – the correct idiom is believe *to be* & not believe *as*

So the correct sentences will read,

A) John has forbidden his daughter to go out in the night.

B) The GMAT comprises AWA, Quant, IR, and Verbal sections.

C) The President of the United States is considered the most powerful person in the world.

D) I believe John's version to be the truth.

An idiom, by definition, is the commonly and universally accepted usage of a group of words that could actually have different meanings when used individually. There is no reason why a particular idiom is correct or incorrect.

While there are more than 15000 idioms in the English language, the GMAT favors only a fraction of these. We have provided on the next page a list of the commonly tested Idioms on the GMAT along with their correct and incorrect usages (wherever applicable). Go through this list and memorize the ones that your ear doesn't recognize.

Note: If you need a more comprehensive idiom list, download the *Aristotle Prep Comprehensive Idiom List* from the **Free Resources** section of our website.

The Aristotle Prep Idiom List

1. **a means to** - something done to achieve something else

   Correct: For some people, laptops are just a means to an end.

   Incorrect: For some people, laptops are just a means for an end.

   Incorrect: For some people, laptops are just the means to an end.

   Note: Do not confuse this with the idiom 'by means of' which means by the use of something.

   (OG 12 – Q 72)

2. **an instance of** – an example of

   Correct: This is a real life instance of piracy.

3. **ability to**

   Correct: Cats have the ability to see in the dark

   Incorrect: Cats have the ability of seeing in the dark

   (OG 12 – Q 51)

4. **accused of**

   Correct: John has been accused of theft

   Incorrect: John has been accused to have committed theft

   Incorrect: John has been accused with theft

5. **act as** - to serve in some special capacity, possibly temporarily

   Correct: Modern mobile phones can act as cameras.

   Incorrect: Modern mobile phones can act like cameras

   (OG 13 – Q 66)
   (OG 12 – Q 65)

6. **act like** - behave in a certain way (will almost always refer to animate things)

Correct: *"Please stop acting like a kid", said the producer to the actor.*

Incorrect: *"Please stop acting as a kid", said the producer to the actor.*

(OG 13 – Q 66)
(OG 12 – Q 65)

7. **aid in** - to help someone in some kind of trouble

Correct: *The motorists needed aid in finding their way out.*

Incorrect: *The motorists needed aid to find their way out.*

(OG 13 – Q 109)
(OG 12 – Q 109)

8. **among X and Y** – to evaluate more than two options

Correct: *John can't decide among a laptop, a mobile phone, and a media player.*

Incorrect: *John can't decide between a laptop, a mobile phone, and a media player.*

9. **appear to be**

Correct: *This dish appears to be undercooked*

(OG 12 – Q 73)

10. **appeal to** - to please or to attract someone

Correct: *Soap operas don't appeal to me.*

Correct: *The idea of taking a vacation appeals to me a lot.*

11. **approve / disapprove of** - to take a favorable/unfavorable view of someone/something.

Correct: *The chairman approves of the new marketing plan*

Correct: *I disapprove of the use of cheating to pass a test.*

12. **as an adolescent/a teenager/a child**

    Correct: As an adolescent, John suffered from tonsillitis.

    Incorrect: While in adolescence, John suffered from tonsillitis.

    (OG 13 – Q 108)

13. **as many/much as** – used to put emphasis on something

    Correct: Jerry made as many as fifteen mistakes in the test.

14. **as many/much X as Y**

    Correct: I have got as many books as you do.

    (OG 12 – Q 76)

15. **associate with -** to be friendly with someone

    Correct: Jacob likes to associate with honest people.

    Incorrect: Jacob likes to associate among honest people.

16. **associate X with Y -** to link someone/something to some other thing or person

    Correct: John always associates coke with pizza

    Incorrect: John always associates coke to pizza

17. **attend to -** to take care of the needs of someone or something

    Correct: Tim is attending to his sick mother

18. **attribute X to Y -** to believe that someone or something is the source of something.

    Correct: We attribute our success to good fortune.

    Incorrect: We attribute our success from good fortune.

    (OG 12 – Q 79, 82)

19. **based on**

> *Correct*: *This movie is based on a true story*

20. **be afraid of**

> *Correct*: *Tim is afraid of the dark.*
>
> *Incorrect*: *Tim is afraid from the dark.*

21. **believe to be**

> *Correct*: *I believe John's version to be the truth.*
>
> *Incorrect*: *I believe John's version as the truth.*
>
> *(OG 12 – Q 45)*

22. **between X and Y** – used to choose between two things only

> *Correct*: *He had to choose between yoga and dance.*
>
> *Incorrect*: *He had to choose between yoga or dance.*
>
> *(OG 13 – Q 44, 93, 95)*
>
> *(OG 12 – Q 44, 96)*

23. **both X and Y**

> *Correct*: *Both John and Jack are coming for dinner.*
>
> *Incorrect*: *Both John as well as Jack are coming for dinner.*

24. **capable of**

> *Correct*: *Jerry is capable of great feats of strength.*
>
> *Incorrect*: *Jerry is capable for great feats of strength.*

25. **centres on** - to focus on someone or something in particular

> *Correct*: *The conversation centered on Mozart's contribution to music.*

26. **choose as** – to select

   Correct: We choose him as our representative.

   Incorrect: We choose him to be our representative.

27. **claim that** – used while proclaiming something

   Correct: Walter claims that he can run backwards.

28. **claim to be** – used while claiming to be some other person

   Correct: The man claimed to be John's long lost son.

   Incorrect: He is claimed as the best athlete of all times.

   (OG 13 – Q 122)

29. **compare to** – mostly used to praise someone by pointing similarities with someone else

   Correct: In Argentina, Maradona is often compared to God.

   (OG 12 – Q 44)

30. **compare with** – used for actual comparison (as we know it)

   Correct: John is comparing a BMW with a Mercedes.

31. **conceive of X as** - to think of someone or something as being someone or something else

   Correct: Jack conceived of a camel as a means of transportation in the desert.

   Incorrect: Jack conceived of a camel to be a means of transportation in the desert.

   (OG 13 – Q 105)

   (OG 12 – Q 106)

32. **concerned with** – involved with or connected to

   Correct: This topic is concerned with the use of DNA sequencing.

33. **concerned about** – worried about

> *Correct*: I am concerned about my brother's health.
>
> *Incorrect*: I am concerned for my brother's health.

34. **conform to** - to agree with or behave within guidelines or regulations

> *Correct*: Does my dress conform to your regulations?
>
> *Incorrect*: Does my dress conform with your regulations?

35. **consequence of** - be the result of

> *Correct*: Rising temperatures are a consequence of global warming.

36. **consider X Y** – think of as

> *Correct*: I consider myself a close friend of the senator.
>
> *Incorrect*: I consider myself to be a close friend of the senator.
>
> *Incorrect*: I consider myself as a close friend of the senator.
>
> *(OG 13 – Q 119)*
>
> *(OG 12 – Q 117)*

37. **contend that** – claim or state

> *Correct*: John contends that his friend is innocent.

38. **contend with** – compete with someone for something

> *Correct*: Jack is contending with Jerry for the award.

39. **contrast X with Y** – compare two dissimilar things which complement each other

> *Correct*: Jenna is contrasting her casual jeans with a formal top.

40. **correlate with** - to match or equate with something.

> *Correct*: The facts don't correlate with her story.
>
> *Incorrect*: The facts don't correlate to her story.

41. **cost(s) associated with**

   Correct: *The costs associated with setting up a factory are prohibitive.*

42. **count on** – depend on

   Correct: *We can count on John to complete the project.*

43. **credited with** – credit person with accomplishment (use this when the *person* comes first)

   Correct: *Newton is credited with the discovery of gravity.*

   Incorrect: *Newton is credited as discovering gravity.*

   Incorrect: *Newton is credited to having discovered gravity.*

   Incorrect: *Newton is credited for discovering the laws of gravity.*

44. **credited to** - credit accomplishment to person (use this when the *accomplishment* comes first)

   Correct: *The team credits its success to good fortune.*

   Incorrect: *The team credits its success with good fortune.*

45. **credit for** – (think in terms of) a credit note

   Correct: *Telenet gave Tim a credit for $100 because of an interruption in service.*

46. **dated at** – to denote a time period

   Correct: *The document has been dated at 100 years old.*

   Incorrect: *The document has been dated at being 100 years old.*

   Incorrect: *The document has been dated as being 100 years old.*

   (OG 12 – Q 78, 140)

47. **date from** - to have an existence that extends from a particular time

   Correct: *These CDs date from the early 70s.*

48. **declared (takes nothing)**

Correct: The monarch declared all fundamental rights unconstitutional.

Incorrect: The monarch declared all fundamental rights as unconstitutional.

Incorrect: The monarch declared all fundamental rights to be unconstitutional.

49. **defined as**

Correct: Evaporation is defined as the process in which water changes into vapour.

Incorrect: Evaporation is defined in the process in which water changes into vapour.

50. **depicted as -** to show someone as something

Correct: The director depicted the actor as a mutant.

Incorrect: The director depicted the actor to be a mutant.

51. **determined by**

Correct: Language structure is partly determined by social structure.

Incorrect: Language structure is partly determined from social structure.

52. **differ/different from**

Correct: Myopia differs from hypermetropia.

Correct: I am very different from my twin sister.

Incorrect: Her hobbies are different than mine.

53. **discourage from**

Correct: I discouraged them from filing a complaint.

Incorrect: I discouraged them to file a complaint.

54. **dispute over**

Correct: There is a dispute over the new name of the city.

55. distinguish X from Y

Correct: *Criminals cannot distinguish right from wrong.*

Correct: *Psoriatic arthritis can be difficult to distinguish from rheumatoid arthritis.*

56. distinguish/distinction between X and Y

Correct: *Criminals cannot distinguish between right and wrong.*

(OG 12 – Q 96)

57. doubt that

Correct: *I doubt that his venture will succeed.*

Incorrect: *I doubt whether his venture will succeed.*

58. dream about

Correct: *All the time I dream about football.*

Incorrect: *All the time I dream of football.*

59. either X or Y

Correct: *I will have either ice cream or pastry.*

(OG 12 – Q 109)

60. encourage X to Y

Correct: *We encouraged Mary to develop her singing talents.*

61. enough to

Correct: *The boy was not tall enough to reach the window.*

Incorrect: *The boy was short enough not to reach the window.*

62. escape from – run away from

Correct: *The thief has escaped from the prison.*

63. **estimated to be**

> *Correct*: *The sculpture was estimated to be worth much more than the base price.*
>
> *Incorrect*: *The sculpture was estimated at worth much more than the base price.*
>
> *(OG 13 – Q 30)*
>
> *(OG 12 – Q 27)*

64. **estimated at** – used to denote the place where the estimation was done

> *Correct*: *The worth of the sculpture was estimated at Madrid.*

65. **expend on** – spend on

> *Correct*: *Don't expend too much effort on this document.*
>
> *(OG 13 – Q 46)*
>
> *(OG 12 – Q 46)*

66. **fascinated by**

> *Correct*: *John is fascinated by his boss.*
>
> *Incorrect*: *John is fascinated with his boss.*

67. **forbid X to do Y**

> *Correct*: *John forbid his driver to enter the house.*
>
> *Incorrect*: *John forbid his driver from entering the house.*

68. **from X to Y**

> *Correct*: *I am travelling from New York to London.*
>
> *(OG 13 – Q 49)*
>
> *(OG 12 – Q 49)*

69.   **in contrast to/with X, Y is....** – On the GMAT both 'contrast to' and 'contrast with' are considered correct

In 'Contrast to', 'contrast' is used as a noun; this is mainly used to show the dissimilarity between two things.

Correct: *John's working style is a contrast to Jacob's.*

In 'Contrast with', 'contrast' is used as a verb and hence denotes the actual act of contrasting two things

Correct:*John is contrasting his working style with that of Jacob.*

70.   **in danger of –ing/danger to**

Correct: *John is in danger of contracting malaria.*

Correct:*Rampant cutting of trees is a danger to the ecology.*

71.   **in order to**

Correct: *She began taking classes in order to learn French.*

Incorrect: *She began taking classes in order that she could learn French.*

72.   **independent of**

Correct: *His reasoning was flawed, and appeared to be independent of any logic.*

73.   **indifferent towards**

Correct: *Can you make yourself indifferent towards someone you love?*

74.   **just as X , so Y** – used to point out similarities

Correct: *Just as Katy is a champion swimmer, so is Angie.*

75.   **less X than Y**

Correct: *My problem is less serious than yours.*

(OG 12 – Q 123)

76. **likely to be**

   Correct: *The CEO is likely to be arrested today.*

77. **localized in**

   Correct: *Are International charities becoming more localized in the economic crisis?*

78. **mandate that**

   Correct: *The rules of war mandate that no prisoner be tortured for information.*

79. **means to an end**

   Correct: *For a lot of people, work is just a means to an end.*
   (OG 13 – Q 75)

80. **mistake X for Y**

   Correct: *John mistook a Ferrari for a Lamborghini.*
   Incorrect: *John mistook a Ferrari as a Lamborghini.*
   Incorrect: *John mistook a Ferrari to be a Lamborghini*

81. **modeled after**

   Correct: *The Indian constitution is modeled after the British constitution.*

82. **more...than**

   Correct: *I am more smart than my brother.*
   Incorrect:*I am more smarter than my brother.*
   (OG 13 – Q 5)
   (OG 12 – Q 4, 99)

83. **native of** – use for humans

   Correct: *John is a native of the US.*

84. **native to** – use for plants or animal species

    Correct: The Royal Bengal Tiger is native to the Sunderbans.

85. **necessary to**

    Correct: The CEO deemed it necessary to ask the employee to resign.

86. **neither X nor Y**

    Correct: We could neither walk nor drive to the venue.

    Incorrect: We could neither walk or drive to the venue.

87. **no less... than**

    Correct: My achievement is no less than his achievement.

88. **not as X but as Y**

    Correct: Edison thought of his unsuccessful attempts to create the light bulb not as failures but as stepping stones to success.

    (OG 13 – Q 15)

89. **not by X....but by Y**

    Correct: The disease is caused not by flies but by mosquitoes

    Incorrect: The disease is caused not by flies but mosquitoes

90. **not only X but also Y**

    Correct: Not only is he very intelligent, but also very humble.

    (OG 13 – Q 4, 64, 86)

    (OG 12 – Q 35, 64)

91. **not so much X as Y**

    Correct: I am not so much sad as perplexed.

    (OG 13 – Q 95)

92. **not X but rather Y**

   Correct: I would have not tea but rather coffee.
   (OG 12 – Q 92)

93. **permit X to Y**

   Correct: John permitted his son to drive to college.

94. **persuade X to Y**

   Correct: I persuaded Tim to complete my assignment.
   (OG 13 – Q 127)

95. **prefer X to Y**

   Correct: Jack prefers tea to coffee.
   Incorrect: Jack prefers tea over coffee.

96. **preoccupied with**

   Correct: The country's mind is preoccupied with soccer.

97. **prohibit X from Y**

   Correct: The landlord has prohibited John from coming late in the night.

98. **pronounced** – declared (when pronounced is used to imply a declaration, then it does not take an 'as')

   Correct: I pronounce you man and wife
   Incorrect: I pronounce you as man and wife
   (OG 13 – Q 47)

99. **range from X to Y**

   Correct: The students' marks range from good to average.

p
149

100. rates for – price of

    Correct: *John enquired the rates for apples.*

101. refer to

    Correct: *My friend referred me to a specialist.*

    Correct: *Evaporation refers to a scientific term.*

    (OG 13 – Q 131)

    (OG 12 – Q 132)

102. regard as – think of

    Correct: *I have always regarded you as my brother.*

103. reluctant to

    Correct: *The child was reluctant to attend the class.*

    Incorrect: *The child was reluctant about attending the class.*

104. restrictions on

    Correct: *The US has imposed restrictions on the licensing of firearms.*

105. seem to

    Correct: *The accused seemed to be hiding something.*

    Incorrect: *The accused seemed like hiding something.*

    (OG 13 – Q 36)

    (OG 12 – Q 35, 72)

106. so X as to Y – used to denote cause and effect. Cannot be used to replace 'in order to'

    Correct: *John's grades are so poor as to lead to his expulsion from the school.*

    Incorrect: *Jack works out every day so as to (in order to) build his stamina.*

107. so X that Y

  Correct: *Jerry is so soft-spoken that one can barely hear him speak.*

  (OG 13 – Q 35, 39, 51)

   (OG 12 – Q 37, 39, 51, 124)

108. so much as – can mean 'but rather'

  Correct: *I'm not looking at him so much as I am studying his jacket.*

  Or, can also mean 'even'

  Correct: *There was not so much as a speck of dust in the house.*

109. **speak from**

  Correct: *The chairman claimed that he was speaking from experience.*

110. subscribe to

  Correct: *I do not subscribe to the view that John is guilty.*

111. such X as Y and Z

  Correct: *This group includes such cars as BMW and Audi.*

112. targeted at

  Correct: *The new ad for lawnmowers is targeted at gardeners.*

  (OG 12 – Q 40)

113. the more/greater X the more/greater Y

  Correct: *The more the prices rise, the more the demand increases.*

114. the same to X as to Y

Correct: This color looks the same to me as it would to anyone else.

(OG 13 – Q 32)

(OG 12 – Q 32)

115. think of X as Y

Correct: John thinks of Jack as his best friend

116. try to

Correct: John said he would try to come on time.

Incorrect: John said he would try and come on time.

(OG 13 – Q 63)

(OG 12 – Q 24, 62)

117. used X as Y

Correct: For centuries, people have been using herbs as remedies for various diseases.

118. unlike X, Y

Correct: Unlike John, Tom wrote a good essay.

Incorrect: Unlike John, Tom's essay was good.

Correct: Unlike John's essay, Tom's essay was good.

(OG 13 – Q 24)

(OG 12 – Q 20, 97)

119. view X as Y

Correct: The management views the problem as an opportunity.

Incorrect: The management views the problem to be an opportunity.

120. whether to

    Correct: John is unable to decide whether to go to Harvard or Stanford. *(wouldn't you want to be in his shoes!)*

121. with the aim of '(verb)ing'

    Correct: Jerry is training for six hours everyday with the aim of winning the marathon.

122. worried about

    Correct: I am worried about my parents.

123. X is to Y what W is to Z

    Correct: You are to your parents what I am to mine.

    (OG 13 – Q 59)

    (OG 12 – Q58)

Style

Style primarily involves the following two aspects – Wordiness and Redundancy

Wordiness

The GMAT likes to keep things simple so all else being equal, a shorter answer is always preferred to a longer one on the GMAT. Thus, if you are totally confused between two options go with the shorter one; statistics suggest that you will be correct more often than not.

For example consider these two sentences:

> 1) John **as well as** Jack reached the office late **on account of** traffic.

> 2) John **and** Jack reached the office late **because** of traffic.

The second sentence sounds much better because it replaces *as well as* with *and* and *on account of* with *because*. The point is that if you can convey the same meaning with one word why use three?

Redundancy

Redundancy basically means saying the exact same thing twice in a sentence. *(By the way did you spot the redundancy in this sentence – **exact same**?)*

Examples:

> 1. *John's marks have **increased up**. (can't increase down can they?)*

> 2. *The **yearly** growth rate is 10% **per annum** (yearly & per annum?)*

> 3. *I have para-glided **previously in the past** (previously & in the past?)*

Keep in mind that *Style* is more subjective than some of the other errors that we have seen in earlier chapters, in the sense that whether a sentence is correct or not will depend on the other options that are available to you. So while *and* is preferred to *as well as*, in case none of the options have an *and* or the option with *and* has some other error, one can easily go with *as well as*.

The good news is that you will rarely be tested only on style; the sentence will usually also contain some other error which will make it easier for you to eliminate the incorrect options.

(OG 13 – Q 28, 52, 55)

(OG 12 – Q 7)

Avoid Slangs and Colloquialisms

Our everyday speech is very informal - full of slangs and colloquialisms – but this should strictly be avoided on the GMAT.

Incorrect: He is really into action movies.
Correct: He likes watching action movies

Incorrect: Jack has been doing theatre for three years now.
Correct: Jack has been involved with theatre for three years now.

Incorrect: It's awfully important that I submit my assignment tomorrow.
Correct: It's very important that I submit my assignment tomorrow

When to Shorten Prepositional Phrases

Consider these two sentences

- *The iphone 5 is available for $199 at Apple stores in the US.*
- *The iphone 5 is available for $199 at US Apple stores.*

The first sentence, by using the preposition *in*, clearly identifies the stores – those owned by Apple in the US. However the second sentence (even though shorter) is ambiguous because *US Apple* could very well be the name of the store, which may very well be located in Japan.

So when is it ok to shorten prepositional phrases and when is it not?

As a general rule, if the preposition in question is *of*, then it is ok to shorten a prepositional phrase; otherwise keep the preposition. However, there can be exceptions such as Q 60 in OG13)

Correct: I liked the last scene of the movie the most (with the preposition 'of').

Correct: I liked the movie's last scene the most (contracted form without 'of').

Correct: John is the son of the senator

Correct: John is the senator's son.

Correct: This apple is sourced from Australia.

Ambiguous: This is an Australian apple (may have been grown outside Australia)

Correct: Tim likes watches made in Switzerland

Ambiguous: Tim likes Swiss watches (may have been manufactured outside Switzerland)

As you may have noticed, the intention is to avoid ambiguity as much as possible. So when confused between two or more options, try to go with the one that is the least ambiguous.

Style and Idioms Practice Drill

1. Roger Federer is considered to be the best tennis player in the world.

2. Roger Federer is regarded as the best tennis player in the world.

3. The per capita consumption of cigarettes in the United States is 10 per person.

4. A low carb diet does not correlate as much to weight loss as does regular exercise.

5. To win the contract, the bidders need to plan out their strategy in advance.

6. On purchase of every laptop, the buyer gets a printer as an added bonus.

7. John did well on the GMAT test.

8. At the end of the wedding ceremony, the priest declared the couple to be husband and wife.

9. Most people associate obesity to a person's desire to consume excessive food, though the problem could sometimes be purely genetic or linked to hormones.

10. The organization where I work provides me with both free lunch as well as return cab fare.

11. I am unable to decide between a pizza or a burger.

12. The teacher has forbidden her students from going out of the class.

13. The company's products are targeted towards senior citizens and not at teenagers.

14. The GMAT comprises of Quant, Verbal, AWA, and, Integrated Reasoning sections.

15. At the end of the conference, the chairman briefly summarized the discussion.

16. The acting style of a lot of modern actors is modeled upon that of greats such as Marlon Brando and Robert De Niro.

17. The more the prices rise, the greater becomes the demand for a wage hike.

18. The Human Resource manager has promised the employees union that he will try and resolve all of its concerns.

19. In the early 1920s, when Temburg was a small, sleepy town, a series of murders shook its residents.

Style and Idioms Practice Drill - Explanations

1. **Correct Answer:** Roger Federer is considered ~~to be~~ the best tennis player in the world.

   Explanation: 'Considered' does not take anything.

   ----

2. **Correct Answer:** The sentence is correct as written. 'Regarded as' is the correct idiom.

   ----

3. **Correct Answer:** The per capita consumption of cigarettes in the United States is 10.
   OR
   The consumption of cigarettes in the United States is 10 per person.

   Explanation: 'Per capita' and 'per person' mean the same thing so the use of both in a sentence is redundant.

   ----

4. **Correct Answer:** A low carb diet does not correlate as much **with** ~~to~~ weight loss as does regular exercise.

   Explanation: The correct idiom is *correlate with* and not *correlate to*.

   ----

5. **Correct Answer:** To win the contract, the bidders need to plan out their strategy.

   Explanation: 'Planning' is always done 'in advance'.

   ----

6. **Correct Answer:** On purchase of every laptop, the buyer gets a printer as bonus.

   Explanation: 'Bonus' by definition is always added or extra.

   ----

7. **Correct Answer:** John did well on the GMAT.

   Explanation: You know what the 'T' in 'GMAT' stands for don't you?

   ----

8. **Correct Answer:** At the end of the wedding ceremony, the priest declared the couple ~~to be~~ husband and wife.

   Explanation: 'Declared' does not take anything.

   ----

9. **Correct Answer:** Most people associate obesity **with** ~~to~~ a person's desire to consume excessive food, though the problem could sometimes be purely genetic or linked to hormones.

   Explanation: The correct idiom is *associate X with Y*.

   ----

10. **Correct Answer:** The organization **in which** ~~where~~ I work provides me with both free lunch **and** ~~as well as~~ return cab fare.

    Explanation: 'Where' is used to refer to a location and cannot be used to refer to an entity 'organization'. Also the correct idiom is both X and Y.

    ----

11. **Correct Answer:** I am unable to decide between a pizza and ~~or~~ a burger.

    Explanation: The correct idiom is *between X and Y.*

    ----

12. **Correct Answer:** The teacher has forbidden her students **to go** ~~from going~~ out of the class.

    Explanation: The correct idiom is *forbid X to do* something.

    ----

13. **Correct Answer:** The company's products are targeted **at** ~~towards~~ senior citizens and not at teenagers.

    Explanation: The correct idiom is *targeted at.*

    ----

14. **Correct Answer:** The GMAT comprises ~~of~~ Quant, Verbal, AWA, and, Integrated Reasoning sections.

    Explanation: 'Comprises' does not take anything.

    ----

15. **Correct Answer:** At the end of the conference, the chairman ~~briefly~~ summarized the discussion.

    Explanation: A *summary* is always brief.

    ----

16. **Correct Answer:** The acting style of a lot of modern actors is modeled **after** ~~upon~~ that of greats such as Marlon Brando and Robert De Niro.

    Explanation: The correct idiom is *modeled after.*

    ----

17. **Correct Answer:** The sentence is correct as written.

    ----

18. **Correct Answer:** The Human Resource manager has promised the employees union that he will try **to** ~~and~~ resolve all of its concerns.

    Explanation: The correct idiom is *try to.*

    ----

19. **Correct Answer:** The sentence is correct as written. 'When' correctly refers to a time period – 1920s.

Meanings

How is 'Meaning' tested on the GMAT?

First of all, let us reiterate that this is not some new error type that the GMAC has suddenly started testing. Meanings have always been tested on GMAT Sentence Correction because there is no way you can arrive at the answer if you don't understand the meaning of the sentence. The only difference is that the stress is much more on meanings now, which is why we have included this topic as a separate section in this book.

So what do we mean by the *meaning* of a sentence?

The meaning of a sentence is whatever information it is that the sentence is trying to communicate to its reader.

As much as possible try to stay with the meaning implied by the original sentence. You can correct the grammatical errors but the meaning that is implied should ideally not change.

Consider the following question:

> *According to leading nutritionists from around the world, <u>there are several benefits of</u>*
> *<u>having your breakfast regularly</u>*
>
> (A) *there are several benefits of having your breakfast regularly*
>
> (B) *there will be several benefits to have your breakfast regularly*
>
> (C) *there were several benefits why you should have your regular breakfast*
>
> (D) *there had been several benefits of having your breakfast regularly*
>
> (E) *there are several benefits of having your regular breakfast*

As always let's start off by trying to split the options. One way of splitting the options in this particular sentence is by using the tense (*are, will be, were, had been, are*). Since the original sentence is in the simple present tense *are* there is no reason why we should change this, so eliminate options B, C, and D.

Now options A and E both are grammatically correct so which one do you go with?

You check the two sentences for the meaning that each is trying to convey:

The original sentence i.e. A uses the adverb *regularly* to modify the verb *having*; hence A is basically saying that you should have your breakfast regularly or every day.

E uses the adjective *regular* to modify the noun *breakfast;* hence E is actually saying that you should have your regular breakfast i.e. the same breakfast that you eat every day. It is not saying anything about whether you should have this breakfast regularly or once a week or once a month.

Thus E distorts the meaning of the original sentence and A is the correct answer.

Important - Sometimes it is possible that the only option that is grammatically correct conveys a meaning that is different from the meaning supposedly conveyed by the original sentence. In such cases you obviously need to go with the grammatically correct option because an incorrect sentence can anyway never convey any meaning.

Let's look at some common ways in which the GMAT can distort the meaning of a sentence:

1) Incorrect use/placement of Modifiers

The best way to distort the meaning of a sentence is by the incorrect use/placement of modifiers. The proximity rule of modification (that we saw earlier) states that a word or a phrase should be as close as possible to the subject that it modifies.

Consider the following sentence:

They noticed a cup on the table made of glass.

Now this sentence can be interpreted in two ways:

Interpretation 1 – The cup is made of glass.

Interpretation 2 – The table is made of glass.

Ideally, in the above sentence, the meaning being implied is the second one because of the placement of the phrase *made of glass* close to *the table*. This is the kind of ambiguity that an effective test taker will be expected to avoid.

If you are trying to convey that the cup is made of glass, then say:

They noticed a cup that was made of glass on the table.

And if you are trying to convey that the table is made of glass, then say:

They noticed a cup on the table that was made of glass.

Again you need to be careful with the use of adjectives and adverbs (both of which are modifiers, as we saw earlier in this book). For example, using the phrase *have your regular breakfast* in place of *have your breakfast regularly* can totally change the meaning of a sentence.

There are certain words that need to be placed in accordance with what they are intended to modify. Some examples include words such as *only*:

- Only John played with the toys *(nobody else played with the toys)*
- John only played with the toys *(he did not do anything else with the toys such as break them)*
- John played with the toys only *(John did not play with anything else)*

   (OG 13 – Q 42, 122, 130)

2) Incorrect use of Conjunctions or Relationship words

Conjunctions can be used in two ways - either to let a thought continue in the same direction or to show a contrast.

For example: *Because John is a good student, he did poorly on the test.*

There is no grammatical error in this sentence but it just doesn't make logical sense because if John is a good student why didn't he do well?

The correct sentence should read:

- *Although John is a good student, he did poorly on the test.*
  OR
- *John is a good student, yet he did poorly on the test.*

In such questions you have to be very careful about whether to go in the same direction as the original sentence or to show contrast.

Sometimes the sentence might not even use conjunctions but might still give you a very subtle hint as to which direction to go in.

Consider this sentence,

> *The employees had nothing but __bad/good__ things to say about their new boss, a novel situation for the otherwise permanently disgruntled group.*

So did the employees have good things to say or bad things?

The use of the phrase *permanently disgruntled or unhappy group* might lead you to conclude that they obviously had bad things to say but note that according to the sentence this is a *novel or new* experience. There's nothing new if a disgruntled group complains or says bad things, so they must be saying the opposite i.e. good things. You'll only grasp this subtle hint if you read the entire sentence properly up front and ponder over its meaning.

Here's one final sentence,

> *Unlike the tiger, the eagle has several characteristics that make it an excellent and most feared predator.*

Everything looks good about this sentence until you realize that the tiger is also an excellent predator. Then why are we using *unlike* at the beginning of the sentence? We should actually use *like.*

> ~~*Unlike*~~ **Like** *the tiger, the eagle has several characteristics that make it an excellent and most feared predator.*

(OG 13 – Q 21, 23)

3) Incorrect Pronoun Reference

While Pronoun Agreement (using a singular pronoun to refer to a singular noun and vice versa) is definitely a grammatical error, the same is not true of Pronoun Reference.

Consider these two sentences:

- *The students came late and so he was punished* (clearly has a grammatical error because one cannot replace plural noun *students* with the singular pronoun *he*; use *they* instead)

- *John bumped into Jack while running in the field and he has been feeling sore ever since* (While one isn't sure who *he* is referring to, notice that this is just a logical error and not a grammatical one; grammatically the sentence is perfectly sound)

4) Incorrect Comparison

A large number of questions that test you on Comparisons actually will have two or more options that are grammatically correct. You need to find the one that is logically correct.

For example:

> *The flowers in my garden are more beautiful than your car.* (there is no grammatical error in the sentence, just a logical one wherein flowers are being compared with a car)

5) Incorrect Parallelism

Often you can get a sentence on the GMAT in which it appears as if the parallelism is correct. However on deeper inspection you will realize that incorrect items have been made parallel.

For example,

> *The price of a meal at the new restaurant is $90 including three starters, drinking two glasses of wine, and having a choice of six desserts.*

If you read this sentence quickly, you may think that the three items – *including, drinking, and having* – are parallel. However, if you try to grasp the meaning of this sentence you will realize that *including* is in fact common to all the three items, so what need to be parallel are – *three starters, two glasses of wine, and a choice of six desserts*.

So the correct sentence will read:

The price of a meal at the new restaurant is $90 including three starters, two glasses of wine, and a choice of six desserts.

Apart from these there are several other ways of distorting the meaning of a sentence. You'll see some of these in the practice question set in this book. One common link amongst all of them, however, will be the fact they will always have at least two options both of which will be grammatically correct. To arrive at the correct answer you'll need to think about the meaning conveyed by the options respectively.

The importance of Meaning on different Error types

The probability of meaning being tested is much higher with certain errors than with others. Meaning will not be very important with errors that are more technical or grammatical in nature (such as Subject verb Agreement) because on such errors it will be almost impossible to come up with two grammatically correct options with different meanings. Here is the likelihood of meaning being tested on each error type we have discussed earlier in this book:

i. **Fragments and Run-on Sentences** – Both of these are technical errors so the meaning will not be very important.

ii. **Subject Verb Agreement** – This is again a technical error so the meaning is not very important

iii. **Tense** – The meaning will be very important on this as in most cases you will only be able to arrive at the answer if you get the meaning right

iv. **Pronoun** – Pronoun agreement and Pronoun case are technical errors so the meaning will not be very important on these. However, meaning will be important on Pronoun reference errors

v. **Modifiers** – The meaning will be very important because, depending on the placement of the modifier, the entire meaning of the sentence can change

vi. **Parallelism** – On questions that are testing you on straight forward parallelism in a series, the meaning will not be very important. However questions in which it is difficult to figure out what aspects to make parallel, the meaning will be very important.

vii. **Comparison** – The meaning will be very important in understanding what items to compare in a sentence

viii. **Idioms & Style** – Idioms are a technical error so meaning will not be very important on these. However meaning can be important in deciding whether a phrase is wordy or redundant.

SECTION 3

Miscellaneous Errors (Usage)

Apart from the major errors that we saw in the previous chapter, there are certain other errors that are also tested on the GMAT from time to time. Let's look at a few such errors:

1) The Subjunctive Mood

Just for the sake of your knowledge, remember that there are three primary moods in English grammar - Indicative mood, Imperative mood and Subjunctive mood.

The GMAT will only test you on the use of the Subjunctive mood, so we'll restrict our scope to this.

The subjunctive mood is used in the following two situations:

Situation 1: *To indicate a hypothetical situation, a wish, or a circumstance contrary-to-fact.*

Situation 2: *To make a suggestion, demand, desire, etc.*

The following rules apply to each of the above two situations respectively:

Situation 1 - When contemplating hypothetical or contrary-to-fact situations, always use *were and would*. Even if the subject is singular you will still use 'were' and not 'was'.

Examples:

1. *If I were rich, I would buy a BMW.*
2. *If petrol were cheaper, I would use my car everyday.*
3. *If I were you, I would contest the elections.*

Situation 2 - Verbs such as *order, suggest, demand, etc.* must be followed by *that* and the infinitive form of the verb being ordered or suggested, without the *to*.

Examples:

1. *The teacher recommended that Jerry be expelled from the class.*
2. *The manager demanded that John show up for work on time.*

So how do you figure out whether a question is testing you on the use of the Subjunctive mood? Here are a couple of tips:

1. Check for words such as *if, wish, etc.* Though these can also be used in the other moods, they are most commonly tested on the subjunctive mood.

2. Ask yourself if the sentence is talking about an uncertainty, a wish, a suggestion, a demand, etc. If it is, most likely you are dealing with the subjunctive mood.

2) Number Agreement

What is wrong with this sentence?

Only those candidates with an MBA degree can apply for this job.

Since the subject is plural *candidates*, you cannot use the singular *MBA degree*; you need to use the plural *MBA degrees* instead. Hence the correct sentence will read:

Only those candidates with MBA degrees can apply for this job.

Such questions are called Number Agreement questions. This is not something usually tested by the GMAT but may be tested in some questions.

Here are two more examples:

- *Incorrect*: Recently there have been several protests against condominiums that do not allow people with a pet to rent apartments

- *Correct*: Recently there have been several protests against condominiums that do not allow people with pets to rent apartments

- *Incorrect*: Students without a valid hall ticket will not be allowed to sit for the exam.

- *Correct*: Students without valid hall tickets will not be allowed to sit for the exam.

3) The use of *Where*

On the GMAT, *where* will always be used to refer to a specific location; for other cases use *in which*.

- *Correct*: *The town where I was born is known for its fishermen.*
- *Correct*: *The town in which I was born is known for its fishermen.*
- *Incorrect*: *The Company where I work has gone bankrupt.*
- *Correct*: *The Company in which I work has gone bankrupt.*

  (OG 13 – Q 102, 103)
  (OG 12 – Q 12, 104)

4) Each Other vs. One another

Each other is used for two things; *one another* for more than two.

- *The two men are pointing out each other's mistakes.*
- *The students are pointing out one another's mistakes.*

5) Whether vs. If

On the GMAT, *If* is used to introduce a conditional idea or an idea that has just one possibility, whereas *Whether* is used to introduce alternative possibilities, usually with *or not* implied or explicitly stated in the sentence.

Consider the following example:

If you study hard you will definitely do well on the GMAT.

In the sentence above, *if* is introducing a single condition (*if you study hard*) that can lead to the desired goal; we can't replace it with *whether* because doing so will totally distort the meaning of the sentence.

Now look at this one:

I can't decide whether to study or to go out with my friends.

Here *whether* is introducing two alternatives and we cannot replace it with *if*.

To make it clearer , here is a sentence in which we've used both *If and Whether* **together:**

You need to decide whether you will be able to control your temper if he asks you to get out of his office.

(OG 13 – Q 34, 78)
(OG 12 – Q 34, 75)

6) Twice and Double

In simple terms, *double* is used as an adjective and *twice* is used as an adverb. So *double* can modify only nouns or pronouns while *twice* can modify everything except nouns and pronouns.

Because of this difference, *twice* has a broader usage then does *double*.

1) Twice can mean two times – I hit him twice.

2) Twice can mean on two occasions - You must exercise twice every week

3) Twice can also mean in two times the quantity – I have twice as many books as you do

As you can see, only in the third case can *twice* and *double* be substituted for each other; in the first two sentences, inserting *double* in place of *twice* makes the sentence sound absurd

Also keep in mind that t*wice* will always be used in relation to something whereas *double* can be used on its own.

For example

- *My salary has doubled in the last two years.*
- *My salary has become twice of what it was two years back.*

In short *double and twice* both are correct but have different usages, so you will not always be able to do a split using these two choices. You'll instead need to look at the rest of the sentence/options and check which ones use twice/double correctly.

(OG 13 – Q 125)
(OG 12 – Q 125)

7) Prepositions or Conjunctions?

We saw what are prepositions and conjunctions in the chapter on Grammar Review, but sometimes a word can act both as a preposition and also as a conjunction. In that case, how do you identify whether you are dealing with a preposition or a conjunction?

Remember that even though inherently both prepositions as well as conjunctions are connectors, prepositions are used to connect a noun element to a sentence whereas conjunctions have the ability to connect two verbs together which means they can actually connect two sentences to each other.

Examples of Prepositions - *on, over, to, from, about, for, against, with, between, but, etc.*

Examples of Conjunctions - *and, nor, but, or, then, for, since, etc.*

As you might have noticed words such as *for* and *but* can act as both Prepositions as well as Conjunctions; then how do you figure out when it's being used as what?

Try this rule - Divide the sentence into two parts (one part before the preposition/conjunction and the other part after that). Now if the two parts make sense on their own then they are two different sentences and we can only use conjunctions to join two sentences so the word in questions is a Conjunction, else it is a Preposition.

Consider the following examples:

1. *I have been living in New York since last year.*

2. *I have been living in New York since I passed my exams.*

Now in the sentences above, the word in question is *since*.

If you break up sentence one across *since*, the two parts are *I have been living in New York* and *last year*. Now while the first part *I have been living in New York* makes sense the second part *last year* makes no sense. Thus *since* is acting as a preposition here connecting the noun *last year* to the rest of the sentence.

Now doing the same thing with sentence two we get *I have been living in New York* and *I passed my exams*, both of which make perfect sense on their own. Thus *since* is acting as a conjunction here joining two sentences.

8) For and Since

With reference to time, *for* and *since* have different connotations. *For* is used to convey duration and *since* is used to convey when a particular action started.

For example,

> *Correct*: *I have been waiting here for two hours.*
>
> *Incorrect*: *I have been waiting here since two hours.*
>
> *Correct*: *I have been waiting here since 2'o clock.*
>
> *Incorrect*: *I have been waiting here for 2'o clock.*

With reference to Tenses, there is an interesting difference between *For* and *Since*. *For* can be used with any tense but *Since* can never be used with the past tense. In fact *since* is almost always used with the present perfect tense. For example,

The use of *For*

> **Simple Past** – *I studied in Boston for five years*
>
> **Past Perfect** – *I had studied in Boston for a year before I moved to New York*
>
> **Simple Present** – *I study for two hours everyday*
>
> **Present perfect** – *I have lived in New York for a very long time.*

The use of *Since*

> **Correct**: I have been waiting here since 10:00 am.
>
> **Incorrect**: I am waiting here since 10:00 am.

9) Like vs. Such As

Is this sentence correct?

> *I want to eat something sweet like a chocolate or a pastry.*

Even though we speak like this in our everyday conversations (*BTW is it 'everyday' conversations or 'every day' conversations?*), what this sentence is implying is that I **don't** want to eat a chocolate or a pastry but something similar to a chocolate or a pastry.

Here's the rule - On the GMAT *like* means *similar to* and *such as* means *for example*

So the correct sentence will read:

> *I want to eat something sweet such as a chocolate or a pastry.*

Important: Even if *such* and *as* are separated in a sentence, the sentence is still correct.

For example:

> *I want to eat some such sweet as a chocolate or a pastry.*

In the sentence above , even though *such* and *as* are separated by the word *sweet*, the sentence is absolutely correct and *chocolate* and *pastry* are examples of sweets that I want to eat.

(OG 13 – Q 1, 138)
(OG 12 – Q 28)

10) The use of Only

Only is an interesting word because it can be used as both, an adjective and an adverb.

For example

- *This is the only car I have. (Adjective modifying the noun 'car')*

- *I only write the articles, I don't create them. (Adverb modifying the verb 'write')*

For GMAT purpose, *only* will always be used as an *adjective* so try to place it as close as possible to nouns and pronouns (and not to verbs).

For example, if you look at Q6 in OG 13 SC chapter (pg 672), almost everyone manages to come down to options A and C. After this, most students arrive at the answer by preferring the use of *ranks* to *has the rank of* and there is nothing wrong with this. However, if you look at the placement of *only* in these two options, in option A *only* is used as an adjective to modify *heart disease and cancer* whereas in option C *only* acts as an adverb to modify the verb *surpassed*. A is obviously the correct answer even from the meaning point of view.

We cannot think of any instance of an official question that has used *only* as an adverb, so if confused, try to use only as an adjective.

(OG 13 – Q 6)
(OG 12 – Q 5)

11) Due to vs. Because of

Is this sentence correct?

> *The physical test was postponed due to the bad weather.*

Even though this might sound correct it is actually incorrect; the correct sentence will read:

> *The physical test was postponed because of the bad weather.*

Rule - On the GMAT *due to* **will NEVER be used to replace** *because of; due to* **can only replace** *caused by.*

Now, in the above sentence, if you were to replace *because of* with *caused by* the sentence would read:

> *The physical test was postponed caused by the bad weather.*

This obviously does not make any sense; hence we cannot use *due to* in this sentence.

However, the following sentence makes sense:

> *The postponement of the physical test was caused by the bad weather.*

In the sentence above, since *caused by* makes sense, we can replace it with *due to.*

> *The postponement of the physical test was due to the bad weather.*

(OG 13 – Q 7, 33)
(OG 12 – Q 6, 33)

12) Less vs. Fewer

If you want to be *less confused* and make *fewer mistakes* then go through this topic.

Rule - *Less* is used with uncountable nouns. Eg - *less water, less happiness, less money, etc.*

Fewer is used with countable nouns. Eg. - *fewer rupees, fewer people, fewer companies, etc.*

Sounds simple enough.

So which of the next two sentences is correct?

1.   *My class has fewer intelligent students.*

2.   *My class has less intelligent students.*

You are probably thinking that since people can be counted, Sentence 1 should be correct BUT in fact both the sentences are correct and are actually saying two different things:

In Sentence one, *fewer* modifies *intelligent students* and basically says that I have fewer number of intelligent students in my class (say 3 out of 10 students)

In Sentence two, *less* is only modifying the adjective *intelligent* and is basically saying that the students in my class have a lower intelligence level in general.

So before you mark an answer, make sure that you understand the meaning of the sentence correctly.

The same rule applies to *much and many* as well. *Much* is used to refer to an uncountable quantity (such as effort, coffee, etc.) and *many* is used to refer to a countable quantity (such as cups, pencils, etc.)

(OG 13 – Q 9, 83, 101)
(OG 12 – Q 102)

13) Greater vs. More

In general *greater than* is used to compare uncountable nouns and *more than* is used to compare countable nouns.

For example:

- **Correct**: My love for swimming is greater than my love for jogging.

- **Incorrect**: My love for swimming is more than my love for jogging.

- **Correct**: I have more horses than you do.

- **Incorrect**: I have greater horses than you do (implying that the horses are greater in size perhaps).

When the subject is 'number' or some other statistic, always use 'greater than'.

- **Correct**: The number of cars in my garage is greater than twenty.

- **Incorrect**: The number of cars in my garage is more than twenty.

14) Will vs. Would vs. Should

Which of these is correct?

1. *I think you will do well on the GMAT*

2. *I think you would do well on the GMAT*

3. *I think you should do well on the GMAT*

It's the first one!

Use **will** to refer to some event that will happen in the future in relation to the present and use **would** to refer to the future in the past.

(OG 12 – Q 67, 122)

Examples

> *I predict that Germany will win the world cup*
>
> *BUT,*
>
> *I predicted that Germany would win the world cup*

Should is very often used incorrectly in English to refer to an event that will or that may happen in the future. On the GMAT *should* is only used to give a recommendation or a suggestion.

In sentence 3 above, it seems as if I am recommending to the student that he does well, whereas it is more of a prediction on my part.

Also remember that *should* will never be used with verbs such as *recommend, suggest, etc.* because it would lead to an error of redundancy since both the words convey the same meaning of tentativeness.

Example

> **Incorrect:** *I recommend that you should come on time*
>
> **Correct:** I recommend that you come on time
>
> *(OG 13 – Q 54)*
> *(OG 12 – Q 54)*

15) Between vs. Among

The simplest of choices but, surprisingly, a large number of students seem to be unaware of the correct usage of *between and among*.

Rule: *Use between when evaluating two options and among when evaluating more than two options.*

> *Examples:*
>
> 1. *John can't decide between a bike and a scooter.*
>
> 2. *John can't decide among a bike, a scooter and a moped.*

Important: Remember that *between* and *among* will ALWAYS take *and* and not *or*. To say that *John can't decide between a bike **or** a scooter* will always be INCORRECT.

16) Use of Apostrophe with Plural words

Consider the following sentences:

> 1. *This is James house.*
>
> 2. *This is James' house.*

If you are trying to state that the name of the house is *James* then the first sentence is correct. However, if you are trying to state that the house belongs to James, then the second sentence is correct.

With plural nouns, to show possession, we use the apostrophe without the '*s*' at the end.

This looks very simple but can confuse you in actual questions.

For example:

> - *My house is bigger than James'.*

You might think that the sentence is incorrect because it compares *my house* with *James* whereas the sentence is absolutely correct because it is actually comparing *my house* with *James' house*

(OG 12 – Q 118)

17) The use of Punctuation

The GMAT will rarely test you on punctuations, except in the case of run on sentences. However, understanding the use of punctuation can help you grasp subtle meaning shifts in a sentence.

For example,
- *The police caught the thief, using night vision glasses.*
- *The police caught the thief using night vision glasses.*

The use of the comma changes the meaning of the entire sentence. In the first sentence the police is using the night vision glasses whereas in the second sentence the thief is using these glasses.

The two punctuations you need to careful about are the comma and the semi colon.

The comma can help you identify modifying phrases or items in a list. Remember that a non-essential modifying phrase will always be set off by commas. Similarly items in a list will always be separated by commas.

>*Correct*: Sam, having won the lottery, decided to buy a yacht.

>*Correct*: Sam is buying a yacht, a sports car, and a villa on the French Riviera.

The semi colon should immediately make you look for run on sentences. For example, if some of the options in a particular question use the comma and some use a semi colon, you should immediately check whether the parts before and after the comma are dependent or independent clauses.

>*Incorrect*: John is here, Jack is also here.

>*Correct*: John is here; Jack is also here.

18) Rather than vs. Instead of

It is extremely unlikely that the GMAT will ask you to chose between two options only on the basis of *rather than* and *instead of*. Usually there will be some other error as well in one of the options.

Still you should know the difference between the two:

Rather than is used to express preference of one thing over another whereas *instead of* is used to replace one thing with another.

> *I will have tea rather than coffee.*

What you are saying is that you would prefer tea but if tea is not available you will be ok with coffee as well.

> *I will have tea instead of coffee.*

Here you are not just expressing preference but rather you are replacing one option with another; so you will not have coffee, but only tea.

Also remember that technically, *rather than* is a conjunction so it can be followed by anything - noun, phrase, clause - whereas *instead of* is a preposition so it can be followed only by nouns.

For example

- *I went in the house instead of in the garden.*
- *I went in the house instead of the garden.*

In Sentence one above, *instead of* is incorrect because it is followed by the phrase *in the garden*. Here the correct usage would be *rather than*.

In Sentence two *instead of* is correct since it is followed by the noun *garden*. Note that *rather than* can also be used in this sentence to replace *instead of*.

19) Subordination and Coordination

We looked at the concepts of coordinating and subordinating conjunctions in the chapter on grammar review. Now let's take a look at how these might be tested on the GMAT.

> **Incorrect**: *High cholesterol content in blood can lead to heart failure and blockage of arteries in the heart.*

The use of *and* here incorrectly signifies that both *heart failure* and *blockage of arteries* are equally important and more importantly, that they could be mutually exclusive whereas the two are actually related in the sense that one is causing the other. Thus we need to subordinate the last part of the sentence to the first part by using a subordinating conjunction such as *by*.

Correct: *High cholesterol content in blood can lead to heart failure by blocking the arteries in the heart.*

Thus, when you want to draw equal emphasis to two parts of a sentence, or coordinate them, you use coordinating conjunctions such as *and or but,* but when you want to emphasize one part over the other, you subordinate one to the other with words such as *although, while,* or *since.*

20) The use of Double Negatives

A double negative occurs when two forms of negation are used in the same clause or sentence.

Examples

- *I don't need no education.*
- *He hasn't done nothing*

A double negative is an absolute no-no on the GMAT.

- **Incorrect**: There were **no** goals **nor** corners in the match.
- **Correct**: There were **no** goals **or** corners in the match
- **Correct**: There were **neither** goals **nor** corners in the match

(OG 13 – Q 21)

SECTION 4

All New Practice Set

Aristotle Sentence Correction Practice Set

1. John, a resident of Lake City and an employee of The Bell Company, <u>is currently working on a new project that will revolutionize the telecommunication industry, which will lead to a lowering of rates for</u> making international calls.

   (A) is currently working on a new project that will revolutionize the telecommunication industry, which will lead to a lowering of rates for

   (B) is currently working on a new project that will revolutionize the telecommunication industry, leading to a lowering of rates for

   (C) which is currently working on a new project to revolutionize the telecommunication industry and also lead to lower rates for

   (D) who is currently working on a new revolutionary project in the telecommunication industry, which will lead to a lowering of rates for

   (E) has been currently working on a new project that will revolutionize the telecommunication industry as well as lower the rates for

2. <u>Cristina started the test later than the rest of the students but was still able to complete it in the allotted time.</u>

   (A) Cristina started the test later than the rest of the students but was still able to complete it in the allotted time

   (B) Cristina started the test later than the rest of the students, however she was still able to complete the test in the allotted time

   (C) Even though Cristina started the test later than the rest of the students, yet she was able to complete it in the allotted time

   (D) Having started the test later than the rest of the students, Cristina was able to complete it in the allotted time

   (E) Cristina was able to complete the test in the allotted time, yet she started it later than the rest of the students

3. Miroslav Klose, with 14 goals to his credit, is the second leading goal scorer in football World Cups, <u>bettered only by Ronaldo's 15 goals.</u>

    (A) bettered only by Ronaldo's 15 goals

    (B) bettered only by Ronaldo, who has 15 goals to his name

    (C) only bettered by Ronaldo's 15 goals

    (D) bettered only by Ronaldo and his 15 goals

    (E) only bettered by Ronaldo, having 15 goals to his name

4. <u>Priscilla and I was punished by the teacher</u> for not completing the assignment on time.

    (A) Priscilla and I was punished by the teacher

    (B) Priscilla as well as me were punished by the teacher

    (C) Priscilla and me were punished by the teacher

    (D) Priscilla as well as I was punished by the teacher

    (E) The teacher punished Priscilla and I

5. The famous actor, whose last three movies <u>were severely criticized both by the critics and the general public for their extremely graphic violent scenes, deciding</u> to work in family dramas only.

    (A) were severely criticized both by the critics and the general public for their extremely graphic violence scenes, deciding

    (B) had been severely criticized by both the critics and by the general public for his extremely graphic violence scenes, has decided

    (C) were subjected to severe criticism by both the critics and the general public for their extremely graphic violence scenes, has decided

    (D) were severely criticized by both the critics and the general public for their extremely graphic violence scenes, decided

    (E) had extremely graphic violence scenes, has been severely criticized by the critics and by the general public, therefore deciding

6. The plantation owners are a worried lot because the rains are just around the corner and <u>neither the topsoil has arrived nor have the plants</u>.

    (A)   neither the topsoil has arrived nor have the plants

    (B)   neither the topsoil has arrived nor the plants

    (C)   neither the topsoil nor the plants has arrived

    (D)   neither of the topsoil or plants has arrived

    (E)   neither has the topsoil nor the plants have arrived

7. <u>As an expert at repairing all kinds of electrical engines, the new project involving the repair and maintenance of pumping motors in all the buildings of the condominium was just the kind of assignment Edward</u> had been looking for.

    (A)   As an expert at repairing all kinds of electrical engines, the new project involving the repair and maintenance of pumping motors in all the buildings of the condominium was just the kind of assignment Edward

    (B)   As an expert at repairing all kinds of electrical engines, Edward regarded the new project involving the repair and maintenance of pumping motors in all the buildings of the condominium as just the kind of assignment he

    (C)   As an expert at repairing all kinds of electrical engines, the new project involving the repair and maintenance of pumping motors in all the buildings of the condominium was considered just the kind of assignment Edward

    (D)   Edward was an expert at repairing all kinds of electrical engines, thus the new project involving the repair and maintenance of pumping motors in all the buildings of the condominium was just the kind of assignment he

    (E)   Edward, as an expert at repairing all kinds of electrical engines, considered the new project involving the repair and maintenance of pumping motors in all the buildings of the condominium to be just the kind of assignment he

8. Automated baggage handling systems <u>are ensuring that by the time a passenger is out of their plane,</u> their baggage is already waiting for them.

    (A)   are ensuring that by the time a passenger is out of their plane,

    (B)   have ensured that by the time a passenger is out of his or her plane,

    (C)   ensure that by the time a passenger is out of his or her plane,

    (D)   ensure that by the time passengers are out of their plane,

    (E)   ensuring that by the time passengers are out of their plane,

9. Although the plastic bag ban in the city is yet to formally come into effect, <u>government agencies have stepped up their drive against it and also issued notices in some cases</u>.

   (A) government agencies have stepped up their drive against it and also issued notices in some cases

   (B) government agencies stepped up their drive against it and also issued notices in some cases

   (C) government agencies have stepped up their drive against the ban and have also issued notices in some cases

   (D) government agencies are stepping up their drive against it, even issuing notices in some cases

   (E) government agencies have stepped up their drive against the use of plastic bags and also issued notices in some cases

10. Jerry knows it is futile to convince his wife to buy the beach house because <u>she is neither fond of swimming nor does she like to surf</u>.

   (A) she is neither fond of swimming nor does she like to surf

   (B) she is neither fond of swimming nor of surfing

   (C) she is neither fond of swimming nor surfing

   (D) neither is she fond of swimming nor of surfing

   (E) neither is she fond of swimming nor does she like to surf

11. <u>London is a city on the move, this makes its airport one of the busiest in the world.</u>

   (A) London is a city on the move, this makes its airport one of the busiest in the world

   (B) London is a city on the move, which makes its airport one of the busiest in the world

   (C) London is a city on the move, a fact that makes its airport one of the busiest in the world

   (D) Being a city on the move, London has made its airport one of the busiest in the world

   (E) London, a city on the move, makes its airport one of the busiest in the world

12. <u>The war veteran remembered meeting the mother of a soldier who had been tortured brutally by the enemy forces during the felicitation ceremony.</u>

    (A) The war veteran remembered meeting the mother of a soldier who had been tortured brutally by the enemy forces during the felicitation ceremony

    (B) The war veteran remembered meeting the mother of a soldier during the felicitation ceremony who had been tortured brutally by the enemy forces

    (C) During the felicitation ceremony, the war veteran remembered meeting the mother of a soldier who had been tortured brutally by the enemy forces

    (D) During the felicitation ceremony, the war veteran remembered meeting a soldier's mother whom the enemy forces had brutally tortured

    (E) The war veteran remembered meeting the mother of a solider during his felicitation ceremony, a soldier who had been brutally tortured by the enemy forces

13. While polarized sunglasses are extremely popular for their anti-glare feature, <u>pilots should avoid using these because their coating will make it almost impossible to read the digital instruments inside the aircraft.</u>

    (A) pilots should avoid using these because their coating will make it almost impossible to read the digital instruments inside the aircraft

    (B) their use should be avoided by pilots because their coating make it almost impossible to read the digital instruments inside the aircraft

    (C) pilots should avoid using it because the coating on these glasses makes it almost impossible to read the digital instruments inside the aircraft

    (D) they should not be used by pilots because of the coating on these glasses making it almost impossible reading the digital instruments inside the aircraft

    (E) they should not be used by pilots because the coating on these glasses makes it almost impossible to read the digital instruments inside the aircraft

14. As people become more and more aware of the dangers of water borne diseases, the demand for mineral water <u>is increasing at a rapid rate, bottled mineral water providing both easy transportability and assured water quality</u>.

   (A) is increasing at a rapid rate, bottled mineral water providing both easy transportability and assured water quality

   (B) has been increasing at a rapid rate, because of bottled mineral water both providing easy transportability and assuring water quality

   (C) has increased at a rapid rate, since bottled mineral water provides both easy transportability and assures water quality

   (D) will increase at a rapid rate because bottled mineral water provides both easy transportability and assured water quality

   (E) increases at a rapid rate, with bottled mineral water providing both easy transportability and assuring water quality

15. The concert rules as defined by the organising committee <u>does not allow the use of mobile phones during the concert nor does it allow the consumption of hard drinks</u>.

   (A) does not allow the use of mobile phones during the concert nor does it allow the consumption of hard drinks

   (B) do not allow mobile phones to be used during the concert, not allowing the consumption of hard drinks as well

   (C) do not allow the use of mobile phones nor the consumption of hard drinks during the concert

   (D) do not allow the use of mobile phones or the consumption of hard drinks during the concert

   (E) neither allows the use of mobile phones during the concert nor do they allow the consumption of hard drinks

16. In one particular species of the Australian parakeet, the male <u>is smaller than the female having red markings all over its feathers</u>.

   (A) is smaller than the female having red markings all over its feathers

   (B) is as small as the female with red markings all over its feathers

   (C) that is smaller than the female and has red markings all over its feathers

   (D) is smaller than the female is and with red markings all over its feathers

   (E) is smaller than the female, with red markings all over its feathers

17. The vendor informed the company that <u>neither of their orders were ready.</u>

    (A)   neither of their orders were ready

    (B)   neither of its orders were ready

    (C)   neither of its order was ready

    (D)   neither of its orders was ready

    (E)   its orders, neither of them, were ready

18. When the results of the final examinations were announced, Susan was surprised to note that she had performed well in <u>both History and Political Science, subjects where she had always struggled, and poor in English,</u> her area of expertise.

    (A)   both History and Political Science, subjects where she had always struggled, and poor in English,

    (B)   History and Political Science, subjects in which she had always struggled, and poorly in English,

    (C)   both History as well as Political Science, subjects in which she had always struggled, and poor in English,

    (D)   History and Political Science, both being subjects where she had always struggled, and poorly in English,

    (E)   subjects where she had always struggled, History and Political Science, and poorly in English,

19. The United States <u>has relaxed overseas borrowing rules for corporates, as a result US based companies will now find</u> it easier to refinance their dollar loans through overseas debt.

    (A)   has relaxed overseas borrowing rules for corporates, as a result US based companies will now find

    (B)   has relaxed overseas borrowing rules for corporates, hence companies in the US will now find

    (C)   has relaxed borrowing rules for overseas corporates, resulting in US based companies now finding

    (D)   relaxation of overseas borrowing rules for corporates resulted in US based companies now finding

    (E)   has relaxed overseas borrowing rules for corporates, so US based companies will now find

20. <u>With a robust economy and well educated and well to do citizens, Zimbabwe was once the success story of Southern Africa, but over the last one and a half decades things have got harder for it as urban areas ceased to create jobs and rural areas felt the pressure as well.</u>

    (A)   With a robust economy and well educated and well to do citizens, Zimbabwe was once the success story of Southern Africa, but over the last one and a half decades things have got harder for it as urban areas ceased to create jobs and rural areas felt the pressure as well

    (B)   Zimbabwe, with a robust economy and well educated and well to do citizens, once the success story of Southern Africa, but over the last one and a half decades things have got harder for it as urban areas have ceased to create jobs and rural areas have felt the pressure as well

    (C)   With a robust economy having well educated and well to do citizens, Zimbabwe was once the success story of Southern Africa, however over the last one and a half decades things got harder for it as a result of urban areas ceasing to create jobs, with even rural areas feeling the pressure

    (D)   Zimbabwe was once the success story of Southern Africa, with a robust economy and well educated and well to do citizens, but over the last one and a half decades things have got harder for it as urban areas ceased to create jobs and rural areas felt the pressure as well

    (E)   With a robust economy and well educated and well to do citizens, Zimbabwe was once the success story of Southern Africa, but over the last one and a half decades things have got harder for it as urban areas have ceased to create jobs and rural areas have felt the pressure as well

21.   <u>If Sam reached the airport in time</u>, he would have been holidaying in Germany by now.

    (A)   If Sam reached the airport in time,

    (B)   If Sam would have reached the airport in time,

    (C)   Sam having reached the airport in time,

    (D)   Had Sam reached the airport in time,

    (E)   Sam, reaching the airport in time,

22.   <u>I had visited Niagara Falls last weekend but nobody believes me when I tell them I did it.</u>

    (A)   I had visited Niagara Falls last weekend but nobody believes me when I tell them I did it

    (B)   I visited Niagara Falls last weekend but nobody believes me when I tell them I did it

    (C)   I had visited Niagara Falls last weekend but nobody believed me when I tell them I did so

    (D)   I visited Niagara Falls last weekend but nobody believes me when I tell them I did so

    (E)   I had visited Niagara Falls last weekend but nobody believes me when I told them I did so

23.   <u>The forests are being cut on a large scale these days, which is a factor contributing to global warming</u>.

    (A)   The forests are being cut on a large scale these days, which is a factor contributing to global warming

    (B)   The forests are being cut on a large scale these days, this is a factor contributing to global warming

    (C)   The large scale cutting of forests these days is a factor contributing to global warming

    (D)   Contributing to global warming, the large scale cutting of forests these days is a factor

    (E)   The fact that forests are being cut on a large scale these days is a factor contributing to global warming

24.   While some may doubt the feasibility of the proposal, <u>it is based on empirical evidence, unlike policies resulting from either fanciful suppositions or as a result of</u> political whims.

    (A)   it is based on empirical evidence, unlike policies resulting from either fanciful suppositions or as a result of

    (B)   it is based on empirical evidence, unlike policies that result from either fanciful suppositions or

    (C)   based on empirical evidence, unlike policies that result from either fanciful suppositions or from

    (D)   because it is based on empirical evidence, unlike policies that result from either fanciful suppositions or

    (E)   it is based on empirical evidence rather than fanciful suppositions or

25. Prices of commercial property have fallen drastically in the country over the last two quarters, as investors, in these uncertain times, <u>prefer holding cash over investing in property</u>.

    (A) prefer holding cash over investing in property

    (B) would much rather hold cash than investing in property

    (C) prefer holding cash to investing in property

    (D) are preferring to hold cash over investing in property

    (E) would much rather prefer to hold cash than to invest in property

26. According to leading economists across the world, rising inflation is one of the <u>factors that seem to indicate that an economy</u> might be headed for a recession.

    (A) factors that seems to indicate that an economy

    (B) factors, which seem to indicate that an economy

    (C) factors that seem to indicate an economy

    (D) factors that seem to indicate that an economy

    (E) factors which seems to indicate that an economy

27. Despite protests by its employees, the company has decided to abolish the trend of giving out bonuses to every member of the staff, <u>stating that henceforth bonuses will be given only to those staff members who</u> achieve more than $100000 in sales every year.

    (A) stating that henceforth bonuses will be given only to those staff members who

    (B) stated that henceforth bonuses will only be given to those staff members

    (C) by stating that henceforth only bonuses will be given to those staff members that

    (D) stating that henceforth bonuses will be given to those staff members who only

    (E) and has stated that henceforth bonuses would be given to those staff members only who

28. In order to reduce light-duty vehicle greenhouse gas emissions, a company <u>can use either low-carbon and renewal power or make land use changes; however, neither of these strategies are by themselves</u> sufficient to achieve success, and must be used together to reduce emissions.

    (A)   can use either low-carbon and renewal power or make land use changes; however, neither of these strategies are by themselves

    (B)   can either use low-carbon and renewal power or make land use changes; however, neither of these strategies are by themselves

    (C)   can use either low-carbon and renewal power or land use changes have to be made; however, neither of these strategies is by themselves

    (D)   can either use low-carbon and renewal power or make land use changes; however, neither of these strategies is by itself

    (E)   can either use low-carbon and renewal power or it can make land use changes; however, neither of these strategies is by itself

29. The users of the new Dell laptop claim that it <u>is much more better, or at least as better, as any</u> of the other laptops currently available in the market.

    (A)   is much more better, or at least as better, as any

    (B)   is much better, or at least as better, as any

    (C)   is much better, or at least as better, than any

    (D)   is much better than any

    (E)   is more better than any

30. The teacher sympathised with the students who were forced to attend classes on Sundays, stating that <u>if he was in charge, he would declare every Saturday and Sunday as holidays</u>.

    (A)   if he was in charge, he would declare every Saturday and Sunday as holidays

    (B)   if he were in charge, he would declare every Saturday and Sunday as holidays

    (C)   he would declare every Saturday and Sunday as holidays if he was in charge

    (D)   if he were in charge, he would declare every Saturday and Sunday holidays

    (E)   every Saturday and Sunday would be holidays if he was in charge

31. The amateur artist created <u>less paintings this year than last year, and now that he has got a full time job, he has even less incentive to do it</u>.

    (A)   less paintings this year than last year, and now that he has got a full time job, he has even less incentive to do it

    (B)   smaller paintings this year than did last year, and now that he has got a full time job, he has even less incentive to do it

    (C)   fewer paintings this year than he did last year, and now that he has got a full time job, he has even less incentive to do so

    (D)   lesser paintings this year than was done by him last year, and now that he has got a full time job, he has even less incentive to do so

    (E)   fewer paintings this year than were created by him last year, and now that he has got a full time job, he has even less incentive to do it

32. The Town and Country Club purchased, for its members, customised golf <u>buggies and 20 sets of the best golf clubs, also organizing training sessions for them with leading professional golfers.</u>

    (A)   buggies and 20 sets of the best golf clubs, also organizing training sessions for them with leading professional golfers

    (B)   buggies, 20 sets of the best golf clubs, and training sessions for them with leading professional golfers

    (C)   buggies as well as 20 sets of the best golf clubs, additionally organizing training sessions for them with professionally leading golfers

    (D)   buggies and 20 sets of the best golf clubs, in addition to organizing training sessions for them with leading professional golfers

    (E)   buggies and 20 sets of the best golf clubs, and organized training sessions for them with both leading as well as professional golfers

33. The Board's response <u>did not surprise Mandy at all; she was, in fact, expecting</u> such a response.

    (A)   did not surprise Mandy at all; she was, in fact, expecting

    (B)   had not surprised Mandy at all; she was in fact expecting

    (C)   had not surprised Mandy at all; she had, in fact, expected

    (D)   did not surprise Mandy at all; she had, in fact, expected

    (E)   did not surprise Mandy at all; because she was expecting

34. Even though <u>many more students are present in the class today than yesterday, this number is still smaller than last week</u>.

    (A)   many more students are present in the class today than yesterday, this number is still smaller than last week

    (B)   many more students are present in the class today than had been yesterday, this number is still lower than last week

    (C)   much more students are present in the class today than yesterday, this number is still lower than the figure for last week

    (D)   many students are present in the class today as compared to yesterday, this number is still less than last week's

    (E)   many more students are present in the class today than were present yesterday, this number is still lower than last week's figure

35. From getting up early in the morning and going for a six mile run to cutting out fried foods completely from his diet to hitting the gym for two hours every day, <u>it was believed by Lawrence that physical fitness was the key</u> to winning an Olympic medal.

    (A)   it was believed by Lawrence that physical fitness was the key

    (B)   Lawrence believed that physical fitness was the key

    (C)   physical fitness was believed by Lawrence to be the key

    (D)   it was Lawrence's belief that physical fitness was the key

    (E)   Lawrence had believed physical fitness to be the key

36. The logistics start-up company, <u>funded by a group of angel investors and looking to make the most of its first mover advantage, has rolled out an aggressive</u> nationwide advertising campaign.

    (A)   funded by a group of angel investors and looking to make the most of its first mover advantage, has rolled out an aggressive

    (B)   funded by a group of angel investors and looked to make the most of its first mover advantage, rolled out an aggressive

    (C)   funding by a group of angel investors and looking to make the most of its first mover advantage, is rolling out an aggressive

    (D)   which a group of angel investors have funded to make the most of its first mover advantage, has aggressively rolled out a

    (E)   having been funded by a group of angel investors and looking to make the most of their first mover advantage, has rolled out an aggressive

37. The Dikes of the Netherlands <u>were built for stopping sea water from flooding the cities</u> and they do.

   (A) were built for stopping sea water from flooding the cities

   (B) had been built for stopping sea water from flooding the cities

   (C) has been built to stop sea water from flooding the cities

   (D) were built to stop sea water from flooding the cities

   (E) had been built to stop sea water from flooding the cities

38. Australia is <u>one of the countries that have imposed sanctions on</u> Iran.

   (A) one of the countries that have imposed sanctions on

   (B) one of the countries that has imposed sanctions against

   (C) one of the countries which have imposed sanctions on

   (D) one of the countries which has imposed sanctions on

   (E) one of the countries that have imposed sanctions against

39. It is ironical that a majority of employees of the automobile company <u>has voted against the resolution, a resolution that was supposedly created to benefit</u> these very employees.

   (A) has voted against the resolution, a resolution that was supposedly created to benefit

   (B) has voted against the resolution, which was supposedly created to benefit

   (C) has voted against the resolution, supposedly created to benefit

   (D) have voted against the resolution, a resolution which was supposedly created for the benefit of

   (E) have voted against the resolution, a resolution that was supposedly created to benefit

40. The double-clutch gearbox of the new BMW M5 offers seamless shifts all the way up to the 7200 rpm mark; 125 mph is reached in just 12 seconds.

    (A) The double-clutch gearbox of the new BMW M5 offers seamless shifts all the way up to the 7200 rpm mark; 125 mph is reached in just 12 seconds

    (B) The double-clutch gearbox of the new BMW M5, offering seamless shifts all the way up to the 7200 rpm mark, can reach 125 mph in just 12 seconds

    (C) The new BMW M5, with a double-clutch gearbox that offers seamless shifts all the way up to the 7200 rpm mark, reaching 125 mph in just 12 seconds

    (D) The double-clutch gearbox of the new BMW M5 offers seamless shifts all the way up to the 7200 rpm mark and reaches 125 mph in just 12 seconds

    (E) The double-clutch gearbox of the new BMW M5 offers seamless shifts all the way up to the 7200 rpm mark, which results in the car reaching 125 mph in just 12 seconds

41. Using the pretext of reviving the flagging economy, several measures have been proposed by the government that threaten to bring back some of the harsh tax provisions abolished in 1999.

    (A) Using the pretext of reviving the flagging economy, several measures have been proposed by the government that threaten to bring back some of the harsh tax provisions abolished in 1999

    (B) With the flagging economy used as a pretext, several measures have been proposed by the government, which threaten to bring back some of the harsh tax provisions abolished in 1999

    (C) Using the pretext of reviving the flagging economy, the government has proposed several measures that threaten to bring back some of the harsh tax provisions abolished in 1999

    (D) The government has used the pretext of reviving the flagging economy, proposing several measures that threaten to bring back some of the harsh tax provisions abolished in 1999

    (E) Using the pretext of reviving the flagging economy, several measures have been proposed by the government, threatening to bring back some of the harsh tax provisions abolished in 1999

42. Despite being rivals on the cricket field, Andrew Flintoff regarded Brett Lee <u>not as an adversary but a friend, a fact that was obvious</u> in the historic Ashes test match between their respective teams in 2005.

    (A)   not as an adversary but a friend, a fact that was obvious

    (B)   not as an adversary but as a friend; a fact that was obvious

    (C)   as not an adversary but as a friend, a fact that was obvious

    (D)   as a friend and not as an adversary, an obvious fact

    (E)   not as an adversary but as a friend, a fact that was obvious

43. Experts suggest that, <u>during the course of one's preparation for the GMAT, as much time be spent on brushing up the basic fundamentals as on mastering the advanced concepts to avoid any unexpected surprises in the end.</u>

    (A)   during the course of one's preparation for the GMAT, as much time be spent on brushing up the basic fundamentals as on mastering the advanced concepts to avoid any unexpected surprises in the end

    (B)   during the course of one's preparation for the GMAT, an equal amount of time be spent on brushing up the basic fundamentals as is spent on mastering the advanced concepts to avoid any unexpected surprises in the end

    (C)   one spend as much time on brushing up the basic fundamentals as on mastering the advanced concepts to avoid any unexpected surprises in the end, during the course of one's preparation for the GMAT

    (D)   as part of the course of one's preparation for the GMAT, the time spent on brushing up the basic fundamentals and the time spent on mastering the advanced concepts be the same to avoid any unexpected surprises in the end

    (E)   while preparing for the GMAT, one spend as much time on brushing up the fundamentals as on mastering the advanced concepts, to avoid any surprises in the end

44. In the 1960 Chile earthquake, <u>at least 6000 people or more are believed to have been killed</u>.

    (A)   at least 6000 people or more are believed to have been killed

    (B)   more than at least 6000 people were believed as killed

    (C)   it is believed that at least 6000 people or more were killed

    (D)   as many as 6000 people were believed to have been killed

    (E)   at least 6000 people are believed to have been killed

45. *Fortune favours the brave* is a mantra that works <u>not just on the battlefields but in the boardrooms</u>.

    (A)   not just on the battlefields but in the boardrooms

    (B)   not just on the battlefields but also the boardrooms

    (C)   on not just the battlefields but also the boardrooms

    (D)   not just on the battlefields but also in the boardrooms

    (E)   not just for the battlefields but also in the boardrooms

46. The student's indifference towards learning was obvious from his attendance record as <u>he had not made any attempt to attend even a few classes</u>.

    (A)   he had not made any attempt to attend even a few classes

    (B)   no attempt had been made by him to attend even a few classes

    (C)   not even a few classes had been attended by him

    (D)   the student had not made any attempt to attend even a few classes

    (E)   he had not made any attempt for attending even a few classes

47. <u>Electronic devices like smart phones and notebooks, which were once considered to be items of luxury, have now become</u> items one cannot do without.

    (A)   Electronic devices like smart phones and notebooks, which were once considered to be items of luxury, have now become

    (B)   Electronic devices such as smart phones and notebooks, which were once considered to be items of luxury, have now become

    (C)   Once considered items of luxury, such electronic devices as smart phones and notebooks have now become

    (D)   Such electronic devices like smart phones and notebooks, which were once considered as items of luxury, now becoming

    (E)   Electronic devices such as smart phones and notebooks, which were once considered to be items of luxury, becoming

48. Zuckerberg has publicly pledged that unlike his other acquisitions, <u>which were quickly absorbed into Facebook, Instagram will be allowed to run independently</u>.

  (A) which were quickly absorbed into Facebook, Instagram will be allowed to run independently

  (B) which Facebook quickly absorbed, he will allow Instagram to run independently

  (C) Instagram will be allowed to run independently instead of being absorbed by Facebook

  (D) which were quickly absorbed into Facebook, Instagram is to be allowed to run independently

  (E) quickly absorbed into Facebook, Instagram will be running independently

49. <u>The newly launched aircraft engine providing a 50% reduction in noise, double-digit improvements in fuel efficiency and environmental emissions has</u> been hailed by the aviation industry.

  (A) The newly launched aircraft engine providing a 50% reduction in noise, double-digit improvements in fuel efficiency and environmental emissions has

  (B) Providing a 50% reduction in noise, double-digit improvements in fuel efficiency and environmental emissions, the newly launched aircraft engine has

  (C) The newly launched aircraft engine provides a 50% reduction in noise and double-digit improvements in fuel efficiency and environmental emissions has

  (D) The newly launched aircraft engine, which provides a 50% reduction in noise and double-digit improvements in fuel efficiency and environmental emissions, has

  (E) Providing a 50% reduction in noise, the newly launched aircraft engine is also providing double-digit improvements in fuel efficiency and environmental emissions having

50. Even though he has been driving a manual transmission car since the past eight months, John still finds it difficult to handle the clutch and ends up stalling the car quite a few times.

 (A) Even though he has been driving a manual transmission car since the past eight months, John still finds it difficult to handle the clutch and ends up stalling the car quite a few times

 (B) Despite having been driving a manual transmission car for the past eight months, John still finds it difficult to handle the clutch and ends up stalling it quite a few times

 (C) Although he has been driving a manual transmission car since the past eight months, John is still finding it difficult to handle the clutch, as a result stalling the car quite a few times

 (D) John has been driving a manual transmission car since the past eight months, but he still finds it difficult to handle the clutch and ends up stalling it quite a few times

 (E) John has been driving a manual transmission car for the past eight months, but he still finds it difficult to handle the clutch and ends up stalling the car quite a few times

51. A recent research has concluded that organically grown fruits and vegetables were, in general, no more nutritious than their conventional counterparts, which tends to be far less expensive, or were they any less likely to be contaminated by dangerous bacteria such as E. coli.

 (A) no more nutritious than their conventional counterparts, which tends to be far less expensive, or were they any less likely to be

 (B) no more nutritious as their conventional counterparts, tending to be far less expensive, nor were they any less likely of being

 (C) not more nutritious as their conventional counterparts, which tend to be far less expensive, or were they any less likely to be

 (D) no more nutritious than their conventional counterparts, which tend to be far less expensive, nor were they any less likely to be

 (E) as nutritious than their conventional counterparts, which tend to be far less expensive, also not likely to be

52. To make salt from sea water, <u>you start by collecting some sea water in a pond and expose it to the sun leading to the formation of brine, which is then drained into harvesting ponds where</u> sodium chloride or common salt finally crystallizes at the bottom of the ponds.

    (A)   you start by collecting some sea water in a pond and expose it to the sun leading to the formation of brine, which is then drained into harvesting ponds where

    (B)   you start by collecting some sea water in a pond and exposing it to the sun leading to the formation of brine, which is then drained into harvesting ponds after which

    (C)   you start by collecting some sea water in a pond and expose it to the sun, which leads to the formation of brine, and then draining it into harvesting ponds where

    (D)   you start by collecting and exposing some sea water in a pond to the sun leading to the formation of brine, which is then drained into harvesting ponds after which

    (E)   you start and collect some sea water in a pond, then exposing it to the sun leading to the formation of brine, which is then drained into harvesting ponds from which

53. Despite having discussed the matter with all his teachers, <u>Lewis is still unable to decide if he should pay more attention to understanding the concepts or to their application.</u>

    (A)   Lewis is still unable to decide if he should pay more attention to understanding the concepts or to their application

    (B)   Lewis is still confused between paying more attention to understanding the concepts or to their application

    (C)   it is still difficult for Lewis decide if he should pay more attention to understanding the concepts or to their application

    (D)   Lewis is still not able to decide whether he should pay more attention to understanding the concepts or to their application

    (E)   there is still confusion in Lewis' mind with regards to understanding the concepts or to their application

54. According to a recent study of home buyers, <u>the location of a house correlates more with its price than with its quality of construction.</u>

   (A) the location of a house correlates more with its price than with its quality of construction

   (B) the location of a house correlates more with its price as does its quality of construction

   (C) the location of a house correlates more with its price than does its quality of construction

   (D) the price of a house correlates more to its location than does its quality of construction

   (E) the location of a house correlates more to its price than to its quality of construction

55. Robert's tutor recommends that, in order to score well on the GMAT, <u>Robert should put in at least two hours of practice every day and not practice questions indiscriminately.</u>

   (A) Robert should put in at least two hours of practice every day and not practice questions indiscriminately

   (B) Robert should put in at least two hours of practice every day and that he should not practice questions indiscriminately

   (C) Robert will have to put in at least two hours of practice every day and not do practice questions indiscriminately

   (D) Robert put in at least two hours of practice every day and that he not practice questions indiscriminately

   (E) at least two hours of practice need to be put in by Robert every day and he does not have to practice questions indiscriminately

56. According to some entrepreneurs, the most difficult choice one has to make while starting a business is between quitting one's day job and concentrating full time on the business, thereby risking one's future, <u>or continuing</u> with one's day job and working part time at the business until it finds its feet.

   (A) or continuing

   (B) and continuing

   (C) or whether to continue

   (D) or that to continue

   (E) and whether to continue

57. Most spiritually inclined people believe that <u>it is more important to be a good individual than being successful.</u>

    (A)   it is more important to be a good individual than being successful

    (B)   it is more important to be a good individual in comparison to a successful one

    (C)   it is more important that one be a good individual as compared to a successful one

    (D)   being a good individual is more important than being a successful one

    (E)   no less significant than being a successful individual is being a good one

58. The doctor suggested <u>that Larry avoids any strenuous activity for the next two weeks and that his bandage is</u> changed every alternate day.

    (A)   that Larry avoids any strenuous activity for the next two weeks and that his bandage is

    (B)   Larry to avoid any strenuous activity for the next two weeks and that he should get his bandage

    (C)   that Larry avoid any strenuous activity for the next two weeks and that his bandage be

    (D)   that Larry should avoid any strenuous activity for the next two weeks and that his bandage should be

    (E)   Larry to avoid any strenuous activity for the next two weeks and have his bandage

59. <u>Be it for losing weight, improving muscle tone, or to widen their social circle,</u> Americans are flocking to gyms like never before.

    (A)   Be it for losing weight, improving muscle tone, or to widen their social circle,

    (B)   Be it to lose weight, improve muscle tone, or widen their social circle,

    (C)   Be it for losing weight, improving muscle tone, or for widening their social circle,

    (D)   Be it losing weight, improving muscle tone, or widening their social circle,

    (E)   Be it to lose weight, improve muscle tone, or to widen their social circle,

60. <u>The books of Chetan Bhagat, which are available in both soft as well as hard cover, are more popular than those of any other Indian writer.</u>

    (A)   The books of Chetan Bhagat, which are available in both soft as well as hard cover, are more popular than those of any other Indian writer

    (B)   Chetan Bhagat's books, which are available in both soft as well as hard cover, are more popular than that of any Indian writer

    (C)   The books of Chetan Bhagat that are available in both soft as well as hard cover are more popular than those of any Indian writer

    (D)   Chetan Bhagat's books, which are available in both soft as well as hard cover, more popular than that of any other Indian writer

    (E)   More popular than any Indian writer, the books of Chetan Bhagat are available in both soft as well as hard cover

61. <u>As demand for the new generation of microprocessors soars, firms manufacturing the older processors reel under losses.</u>

    (A)   As demand for the new generation of microprocessors soars, firms manufacturing the older processors reel under losses

    (B)   As demand for the new generation of microprocessors soar, firms manufacturing the older processors have been reeling under losses

    (C)   As demand for the new generation of microprocessors has soared, the older processor manufacturing firms reeled under losses

    (D)   As demand for the new generation of microprocessors soars, firms manufacturing the older processors have reeled under losses

    (E)   Owing to the demand for the new generation of microprocessors soaring, firms manufacturing the older processors reeling under losses

62. The minister <u>had expected brickbats, complaints, and pessimism, instead what greeted him was bouquets, praise, and optimism</u>.

    (A)   had expected brickbats, complaints, and pessimism, instead what greeted him was bouquets, praise, and optimism

    (B)   was expecting brickbats, complaints, and pessimism, and was greeted by bouquets, praise, and optimism

    (C)   had expected brickbats, complaints, and pessimism; instead he was greeted by bouquets, praise, and optimism

    (D)   expected brickbats, complaints, and pessimism, however what greeted him was bouquets, praise, and optimism

    (E)   expecting brickbats, complaints, and pessimism, was instead greeted by bouquets, praise, and optimism

63. As part of its growth strategy, <u>the company is looking to apply global strategies using local insights along with expanding their geographical reach</u>.

    (A)   the company is looking to apply global strategies using local insights along with expanding their geographical reach

    (B)   the company's plan is to apply global strategies using local insights and to expand its geographical reach

    (C)   the company, in addition to expanding its geographical reach, is also looking to apply global strategies using local insights

    (D)   the company is looking at applying global strategies and expanding its geographical reach, using local insights

    (E)   the company's plans are for applying global strategies, using local insights, and expanding its geographical reach

64. <u>Iran that has the world's fourth-largest oil reserves also has the world's second-largest natural gas reserves.</u>

    (A)   Iran that has the world's fourth-largest oil reserves also has the world's second-largest natural gas reserves

    (B)   Iran has the world's fourth-largest oil reserves as well as having the second-largest natural gas reserves

    (C)   Iran has the world's fourth-largest oil reserves and second-largest natural gas reserves

    (D)   Iran has the world's fourth-largest oil reserves; the world's second-largest natural gas reserves are also in Iran

    (E)   Iran, having the world's fourth-largest oil reserves, is in addition having its second-largest natural gas reserves as well

65. The policy of "Nationalism" has been around since 1975, <u>when officials in the country—many of whom equate patriotism with supporting the government's policies—began to worry in earnest about whether</u> the country's citizens were patriotic enough.

    (A)   when officials in the country—many of whom equate patriotism with supporting the government's policies—began to worry in earnest about whether

    (B)   when officials in the country—many of them equating patriotism with supporting the government's policies—began to worry in earnest if

    (C)   when officials in the country who equate patriotism with supporting the government's policies begun worrying in earnest if

    (D)   when officials in the country—many of which equate patriotism with supporting the government's policies—begun worrying in earnest whether

    (E)   when officials in the country—many of whom equate patriotism with supporting the government's policies—begun worrying in earnest whether

66. The rise in the level of pollutants in the Yangtze River is almost <u>equivalent to the level of pollutants in</u> the Ohio River.

    (A)   equivalent to the level of pollutants in

    (B)   the same as that in the level of pollutants in

    (C)   the same as the level of pollutants in

    (D)   equal to that of

    (E)   the equivalent of that in

67. Traditional art and modern art, <u>both part of the cultural frame of reference of most Americans and Europeans</u>, share many aspects of the artistic language.

    (A)   both part of the cultural frame of reference of most Americans and Europeans

    (B)   are both part of the cultural frame of reference of most Americans and Europeans

    (C)   part of both the cultural frame of reference of most Americans and Europeans

    (D)   being part of the cultural reference frame of most Americans and Europeans

    (E)   have both been part of the cultural frame of reference of most Americans and Europeans

68. In ancient times tanning, the process of treating animal skin with chemical compounds to produce leather, <u>was considered to be a noxious or odoriferous trade and relegated to the outskirts of</u> town, amongst the poor.

    (A)   was considered to be a noxious or odoriferous trade and relegated to the outskirts of

    (B)   was considered a noxious or odoriferous trade and relegated to the outskirts of

    (C)   was regarded to be a noxious or odoriferous trade, relegating it to the outskirts of

    (D)   had been regarded as a noxious or odoriferous trade and relegated to the outskirts of

    (E)   was considered as a noxious or odoriferous trade, which relegated it to the outskirts of

69. In order to detect cancer early, <u>the awareness of cancer screening and diagnostic tests is a must.</u>

    (A)   the awareness of cancer screening and diagnostic tests is a must

    (B)   it is important to be aware of cancer screening and diagnostic tests

    (C)   one must be aware of cancer screening and diagnostic tests

    (D)   one must have awareness of cancer screening and diagnostic tests

    (E)   it is important that one be aware of cancer screening and diagnostic tests

70. <u>The belief, in some cultures, about the black cat as being a symbol of evil and a harbinger of doom is a relatively recent phenomenon;</u> all cats, including black ones, were held in high esteem among the ancient Egyptians and protected by law from injury and death.

  (A)   The belief, in some cultures, about the black cat as being a symbol of evil and a harbinger of doom is a relatively recent phenomenon;

  (B)   Some cultures' belief about the black cat as a symbol of evil and a harbinger of doom is a relative recent phenomenon;

  (C)   The belief, in some cultures, that the black cat is a symbol of evil and a harbinger of doom   is a relatively recent phenomenon;

  (D)   The belief about the black cat as being a symbol of evil and a harbinger of doom is a relatively recent phenomenon in some cultures;

  (E)   The black cat is believed to be a symbol of evil and a harbinger of doom, this being a relatively recent phenomenon in some cultures;

71. <u>Constructed by the Suez Canal Company and connected the Mediterranean Sea and the Red sea, November 1869 is when the Suez Canal was opened to traffic.</u>

  (A)   Constructed by the Suez Canal Company and connected the Mediterranean Sea and the Red sea, November 1869 is when the Suez Canal was opened to traffic

  (B)   The Suez Canal, constructed by the Suez Canal Company and connecting the Mediterranean Sea and the Red sea, was opened to traffic in November 1869.

  (C)   Having been constructed by the Suez Canal Company and connecting the Mediterranean Sea and the Red sea, Suez Canal was opened to traffic in November 1869

  (D)   The Suez Canal, which was constructed by the Suez Canal Company connecting the Mediterranean Sea and the Red sea, was opened to traffic in November 1869

  (E)   Constructed by the Suez Canal Company and connecting the Mediterranean Sea and the Red sea, the Suez Canal had been opened to traffic in November 1869

72. <u>The absence of an atmosphere and the presence of water is an interesting characteristic of the moon.</u>

    (A)   The absence of an atmosphere and the presence of water is an interesting characteristic of the moon

    (B)   The absence of an atmosphere and the presence of water are an interesting characteristic of the moon

    (C)   The absence of an atmosphere as well as the presence of water are interesting characteristics of the moon

    (D)   An interesting characteristic of the moon are the absence of an atmosphere and the presence of water

    (E)   The absence of an atmosphere and the presence of water are interesting characteristics of the moon

73. The <u>seeming unlimited supply of fresh water and the apparently absent government regulations makes</u> the Canary Island a popular choice for those wanting to buy their own private island.

    (A)   seeming unlimited supply of fresh water and the apparently absent government regulations makes

    (B)   seeming unlimited supply of fresh water and the apparent absence of government regulations make

    (C)   seeming unlimited fresh water supply and the apparent absent government regulations make

    (D)   seemingly unlimited supply of fresh water and the apparently absent government regulations makes

    (E)   seemingly unlimited supply of fresh water and the apparent absence of government regulations make

74. The purpose of the vehicle driving test is <u>to assess a person's ability of recognizing the different traffic signs as well as of his ability to steer</u> and control a moving vehicle.

   (A) to assess a person's ability of recognizing the different traffic signs as well as of his ability to steer

   (B) to assess a person's ability to recognize the different traffic signs as well as to steer

   (C) to be able to assess a person's ability of recognizing the different traffic signs as well as of steering

   (D) for assessing a person's ability to recognize the different traffic signs as well as to steer

   (E) that it can assess a person's ability for recognizing the different traffic signs as well of his ability for steering

75. The government has mandated <u>people living below the poverty line to be provided with meals twice a day and their children to be</u> provided access to free education in publicly funded schools.

   (A) people living below the poverty line to be provided with meals twice a day and their children to be

   (B) that people living below the poverty line should be provided with meals twice a day and their children should be

   (C) for people living below the poverty line meals twice a day and for their children

   (D) people living below the poverty line that they will be provided with meals twice a day and their children be

   (E) that people living below the poverty line be provided with meals twice a day and that their children be

76. While investigating the reasons behind the bankruptcy of the trading company, the empowered committee realized <u>that the company collapsed more due to poor management of funds than due to customers not buying the company's products.</u>

   (A)   that the company collapsed more due to poor management of funds than due to customers not buying the company's products

   (B)   that the collapse was caused more by the poor management of funds than due to customers not buying the company's products

   (C)   that the company collapsed more because of poor management of funds than because of customers not buying its products

   (D)   that the collapse was more due to poor management of funds than because of customers not buying the company's products

   (E)   that poor management of funds did more to cause the collapse than did customers by not buying the company's products

77.   The company has three divisions, <u>each of which specialise in a particular business area.</u>

   (A)   each of which specialise in a particular business area

   (B)   which specialises in particular business areas

   (C)   they specialise in a particular business area each

   (D)   all of them specialise in a particular business area

   (E)   each of which specialises in a particular business area

78.   Differential pricing of gasoline, <u>with a higher price charged to those who can afford it, has often been suggested by experts but it is very tough implementing it.</u>

   (A)   with a higher price charged to those who can afford it, has often been suggested by experts but it is very tough implementing it

   (B)   is a higher price charged to those who can afford it, having often been suggested by experts but being very tough to implement

   (C)   being a higher price charged to those that can afford it, has often been suggested by experts but its implementation is very tough

   (D)   with a higher price charged to those who can afford it, has often been suggested by experts but is very tough to implement

   (E)   with a higher price charged to them who can afford the price, often been suggested by experts but is very tough to implementing it

79. <u>In a move that delighted their shareholders as much as distressed their competitors, the two shipping companies decided to merge, and this led</u> to the formation of the second largest shipping company in the world.

     (A)   In a move that delighted their shareholders as much as distressed their competitors, the two shipping companies decided to merge, and this led

     (B)   In a delightful move for their shareholders and a distressful one for their competitors, it has been decided by the two shipping companies to merge, leading

     (C)   In a move delighting their shareholders as much as distressing their competitors, the two shipping companies decided to merge, which led

     (D)   In a move that delighted their shareholders as much as it distressed their competitors, the two shipping companies decided to merge, leading

     (E)   The two shipping companies, in a move that delighted their shareholders and distressed their competitors, decided to merge and to lead

80. According to industry experts, the biggest difference between colleges <u>in America and colleges in developing countries like India is that in America they are searching for students whereas in India they are searching for faculty.</u>

     (A)   in America and colleges in developing countries like India is that in America they are searching for students whereas in India they are searching for faculty

     (B)   in America and developing countries like India is that American colleges are searching for students whereas in India they are searching for faculty

     (C)   in America and colleges in developing countries such as India is that in America they are searching for students whereas Indian colleges are searching for faculty

     (D)   in America and those in developing countries such as India is that American colleges are searching for students whereas Indian colleges are searching for faculty

     (E)   in America and such developing countries as India is that in America the colleges are searching for students whereas Indian colleges are searching for faculty

81. In order to improve the aesthetics of the neighbourhood, <u>a group of citizens have suggested that the park be not only cleaned but also beautified.</u>

   (A)   a group of citizens have suggested that the park be not only cleaned but also beautified

   (B)   a group of citizens have suggested that the park not only be cleaned but also beautified

   (C)   the park should not only be cleaned but also beautified, a group of citizens has suggested

   (D)   a group of citizens has suggested that the park be not only cleaned but that it also be beautified

   (E)   a group of citizens has suggested that the park be not only cleaned but also beautified

82. In modern supermarkets, <u>a customer does not have to stand in long billing queues if they have purchased ten items or less</u> as there is a separate, dedicated billing queue for such customers.

   (A)   a customer does not have to stand in long billing queues if they have purchased ten items or less

   (B)   customers do not have to stand in long billing queues if they have purchased ten items or less

   (C)   a customer does not have to stand in long billing queues if purchasing ten items or lesser

   (D)   long queues can be avoided by customers who purchase ten or less items

   (E)   customers do not have to stand in long billing queues if they have purchased up to ten items

83. The reason most new ventures fail within a year of their launch is <u>because the founders spend most of their efforts on formulating strategy rather than</u> implementing it.

   (A)   because the founders spend most of their efforts on formulating strategy rather than

   (B)   because the founders are spending most of their efforts towards strategy formulation rather than

   (C)   that the founders spend most of their efforts on formulating strategy rather than on

   (D)   that the founders have spent most of their efforts on strategy formulation instead of

   (E)   that most of the efforts of the founders are spent towards formulating strategy rather than towards

84. Boris Becker, a six-time Grand Slam singles champion, <u>won</u> another 49 singles titles over a career that spanned 14 years.

    (A)   won

    (B)   has won

    (C)   having won

    (D)   winning

    (E)   had won

85. <u>The artist was so famous as to barely being able to step out of his house without being</u> accosted by fans and photographers.

    (A)   The artist was so famous as to barely being able to step out of his house without being

    (B)   Such was the artist's fame that he could barely not step out of his house before he was

    (C)   The artist was so famous that he could barely step out of his house without being

    (D)   The artist, so famous that he was barely able to step out of his house, being

    (E)   No sooner did the artist step out of his house, such was his fame, than he was

86. <u>Unlike writing for magazines, where editors have days, even weeks, to edit copy and proofread, newspaper editors work on daily deadlines.</u>

    (A)   Unlike writing for magazines, where editors have days, even weeks, to edit copy and proofread, newspaper editors work on daily deadlines

    (B)   Unlike writing for magazines, for which editors have days, even weeks, to edit copy and proofread, newspaper editors work on daily deadlines

    (C)   Unlike magazine editors, where they have days, even weeks, to edit copy and proofread, newspaper editors work on daily deadlines

    (D)   Unlike editing magazines, a task for which editors have days, even weeks, to edit copy and proofread, newspaper editors work on daily deadlines

    (E)   Unlike magazine editors, who have days, even weeks, to edit copy and proofread, newspaper editors work on daily deadlines

87. The employees in our organization, <u>unlike that in your organization, are forbidden from discussing</u> client names or activities outside the office.

    (A)   unlike that in your organization, are forbidden from discussing

    (B)   contrasted to ones in your organization, are forbidden to discussing

    (C)   unlike them in your organization, are forbidden to discuss

    (D)   unlike those in your organization, are forbidden to discuss

    (E)   unlike the employees in your organization, are forbidden from discussing

88. <u>It took Abraham less hours and cups of coffee to complete the project than Andy</u>.

    (A)   It took Abraham less hours and cups of coffee to complete the project than Andy

    (B)   Abraham took fewer hours and less cups of coffee to complete the project than did Andy

    (C)   It took Abraham less time and fewer cups of coffee to complete the project than did Andy

    (D)   It took Abraham less time and fewer cups of coffee to complete the project than Andy

    (E)   It took Abraham fewer hours and fewer cups of coffee to complete the project than it took Andy

89. The management was impressed by the fact that <u>even though John had prepared a very comprehensive report, it was presented by him in a very concise manner</u>.

    (A)   even though John had prepared a very comprehensive report, it was presented by him in a very concise manner

    (B)   although John prepared a very comprehensive report, yet he presented it in a very concise manner

    (C)   even though John had prepared a very comprehensive report, he presented it in a very concise manner

    (D)   John had prepared a very comprehensive report, presenting it in a very concise manner

    (E)   John had prepared and presented a very comprehensive and concise report

90. Manufacturers of a new exercise machine claim that it is much more comfortable to use than older machines and hence will encourage people to exercise for <u>longer durations; however, their users state that they do not find the new machine any different from</u> the older ones.

   (A)   longer durations; however, their users state that they do not find the new machine any different from

   (B)   longer durations; however, its users state that they do not find the new machine any different from

   (C)   longer durations; however, the users of this new machine state that they do not find the new machine any different than

   (D)   longer durations; nevertheless, their users state that they do not find the new machine any different from

   (E)   longer durations, however, their users state that they do not find the new machine any different than

91. By Friday evening, the proposal <u>had been signed by over 1000 supporters, many of them has</u> left messages on the page.

   (A)   had been signed by over 1000 supporters, many of them has

   (B)   was signed by over 1000 supporters, many of them having had

   (C)   had been signed by over 1000 supporters, many of whom have

   (D)   had been signed by over 1000 supporters, many of whom

   (E)   was signed by over 1000 supporters, and many of them

92. During his research on modern production systems, workers at a leading automobile manufacturing firm told Professor Roberts that these systems end up encouraging temporary or contract employment and reducing their quality of life.

    (A)   During his research on modern production systems, workers at a leading automobile manufacturing firm told Professor Roberts that these systems end up encouraging temporary or contract employment and reducing their quality of life

    (B)   Modern production systems were encouraging temporary or contract employment and reducing their quality of life was told to Professor Roberts by the workers at a leading automobile manufacturing firm

    (C)   Professor Roberts was told by workers at a leading automobile manufacturing firm that these systems ended up encouraging temporary or contract employment and reducing their quality of life, during his research on modern production systems

    (D)   During his research on modern production systems, Professor Roberts was told by workers at a leading automobile manufacturing firm that they were meant to encourage temporary or contract employment at the same time reducing their quality of life

    (E)   Professor Roberts, during his research on modern production systems, was told by workers at a leading automobile manufacturing firm that these systems ended up encouraging temporary or contract employment and reducing their quality of life

93. The city disaster management corporation has recommended that all residents staying close to the beach should vacate their homes until the tsunami threat passes.

    (A)   that all residents staying close to the beach should vacate their homes

    (B)   all residents staying close to the beach that they should vacate their homes

    (C)   all residents staying close to the beach to vacate their homes

    (D)   that all residents staying close to the beach vacate their homes

    (E)   that all residents staying close to the beach must vacate their homes

94. The restructuring agency <u>explored several alternatives, including complete and partial liquidation of assets, but has not found</u> any feasible solution to the problems faced by the company.

     (A)   explored several alternatives, including complete and partial liquidation of assets, but has not found

     (B)   had explored several alternatives, which include complete and partial liquidation of assets, but has not found

     (C)   explored several alternatives, including complete and partial liquidation of assets, but did not found

     (D)   has explored several alternatives, including complete and partial liquidation of assets, but has not found

     (E)   has explored several alternatives, including complete and partial liquidation of assets, but did not find

95. <u>The abundant supply of fresh water and its location, an isolated landmass in the North Atlantic, makes Iceland a natural nesting location for migratory birds</u>.

     (A)   The abundant supply of fresh water and its location, an isolated landmass in the North Atlantic, makes Iceland a natural nesting location for migratory birds

     (B)   The abundant supply of fresh water as well as its location, an isolated landmass in the North Atlantic, makes Iceland a natural nesting location for migratory birds

     (C)   An isolated landmass in the North Atlantic, Iceland has an abundant supply of fresh water which, along with its location, make Iceland a natural nesting location for migratory birds

     (D)   Its location, an isolated landmass in the North Atlantic, and an abundant supply of fresh water make Iceland a natural nesting location for migratory birds

     (E)   Iceland, having an abundant supply of fresh water and location, an isolated landmass in the North Atlantic, is a natural nesting location for migratory birds

96. The country's policy makers have been severely criticised over the past three years <u>in failing to curb corruption, improving governance, and devising policies to create more jobs.</u>

   (A) in failing to curb corruption, improving governance, and devising policies to create more jobs

   (B) because they have failed to curb corruption or improve governance, not devising policies to create more jobs

   (C) for failing to curb corruption, improving governance, and devising policies to create more jobs

   (D) for failing to curb corruption, improve governance, and devise policies to create more jobs

   (E) for failing to curb corruption and improving governance and also to devise policies to create more jobs

97. According to a popular announcement at subway stations, one is not supposed <u>to smoke, drink, eat, and play loud music either aboard the train or station platforms.</u>

   (A) to smoke, drink, eat, and play loud music either aboard the train or station platforms

   (B) to smoke, drink, eat, and to play loud music either aboard the train or station platforms

   (C) to smoke, drink, eat, or play loud music either aboard the train or on station platforms

   (D) to smoke, to drink, to eat, and play loud music either aboard the train or on station platforms

   (E) to smoke, drink, eat, or play loud music either aboard the train or station platforms

98. <u>The shareholders of the company as well as its Board of Directors have agreed to implement</u> the new cost cutting measures that are expected to result in savings of at least three million dollars per quarter.

   (A) The shareholders of the company as well as its Board of Directors have agreed to implement

   (B) The shareholders of the company as well as its Board of Directors has agreed to implement

   (C) It has been agreed by the shareholders of the company as well as by its Board of Directors for implementing

   (D) The shareholders of the company together with its Board of Directors has agreed towards implementing

   (E) The shareholders of the company and its Board of Directors has agreed to implement

99. According to the public prosecutor, the accused has been charged with siphoning off millions from the treasury, invented fictitious deals, and lied to his superiors.

 (A) with siphoning off millions from the treasury, invented fictitious deals, and lied to his superiors

 (B) for having siphoned off millions from the treasury, invented fictitious deals, and lied to his superiors

 (C) for siphoning off millions from the treasury, inventing fictitious deals as well as lying to his superiors

 (D) with siphoning off millions from the treasury, for inventing fictitious deals, and for having lied to his superiors

 (E) with siphoning off millions from the treasury, inventing fictitious deals, and lying to his superiors

100. Every one of the support staff and the participants have to compulsorily go through a full body search before they enter the competition area.

 (A) have to compulsorily go through a full body search before they enter

 (B) have to go through a compulsorily full body search before entering

 (C) have to compulsorily go through a full body search before he or she enters

 (D) has to compulsorily go through a full body search before entering

 (E) has to compulsorily go through a full body search before they enter

101. Modern zoos cater not only to the recreational needs of people, but also help in conducting research and conservation of wild animals.

 (A) cater not only to the recreational needs of people, but also help in conducting research and conservation of

 (B) cater not only to the recreational needs of people, but also aid in conducting research and in conservation of

 (C) not only cater to the recreational needs of people, but also help to conduct research on and to conserve

 (D) not only caters to the recreational needs of people, but also aid in conducting research and conservation of

 (E) not only cater to the recreational needs of people, but also help in conducting research on and conservation of

102. To appear fashionable, some men wear French cuff dress shirts with jeans or casual clothing, but usually they are worn with a stylish sporty coat or a suit.

  (A) To appear fashionable, some men wear French cuff dress shirts with jeans or casual clothing, but usually they are worn with a stylish sporty coat or a suit

  (B) Although some men, to appear fashionable, wear French cuff dress shirts with jeans or casual clothing, but usually they are worn with a stylish sporty coat or a suit

  (C) Some men, to appear fashionable, wear French cuff dress shirts with jeans or casual clothing, but they are usually worn with a stylish sporty coat or a suit

  (D) To appear fashionable, some men wear French cuff dress shirts with jeans or casual clothing, but these shirts are usually worn with a stylish sporty coat or a suit

  (E) Even though they are usually worn with a stylish sporty coat or a suit, some men, to appear fashionable, wear French cuff dress shirts with jeans or casual clothing

103. One of the artefacts that have been excavated from the recently discovered archaeological site are estimated at being more than 2000 years old.

  (A) have been excavated from the recently discovered archaeological site are estimated at being

  (B) have been excavated from the recently discovered archaeological site are estimated to be

  (C) has been excavated from the recently discovered archaeological site is estimated at

  (D) have been excavated from the recently discovered archaeological site is estimated to be

  (E) has been excavated from the recently discovered archaeological site is estimated to be

104. The charitable trust disbursed 8.7 million dollars in loans over the course of the last one year, however, now they don't remember who they gave it to.

  (A) however, now they don't remember who they gave it to

  (B) however, now they don't remember whom they gave the loans to

  (C) however, now they don't remember who it gave it to

  (D) but now it doesn't remember whom it gave them to

  (E) but now it doesn't remember who it gave the loans to

105. <u>Having toiled tirelessly under the scorching sun for six straight hours, the woodcutter decided to lay down and rest for a while.</u>

    (A)   Having toiled tirelessly under the scorching sun for six straight hours, the woodcutter decided to lay down and rest for a while

    (B)   Having toiled tirelessly under the scorching sun for six straight hours, the woodcutter decided to lie down and to rest for a while

    (C)   Having toiled tirelessly under the scorching sun for six straight hours, the woodcutter, decided to lay down and to rest for a while

    (D)   The woodcutter, having toiled tirelessly under the scorching sun for six straight hours, decided to lie down and rest for a while

    (E)   The woodcutter toiled tirelessly under the scorching sun for six straight hours, decided to lie down and rest for a while

106. The illegal addition of two floors <u>are not the only trouble the hotel could face, it also owes millions in unpaid taxes to the exchequer along with two other hotels.</u>

    (A)   are not the only trouble the hotel could face, it also owes millions in unpaid taxes to the exchequer along with two other hotels

    (B)   is not the only trouble the hotel could face, and it also owes millions in unpaid taxes to the exchequer along with two other hotels

    (C)   is not the only trouble the hotel could face; it also owes, along with two other hotels, millions in unpaid taxes to the exchequer

    (D)   are not the only troubles the hotel could face, it as well as two other hotels also owe millions in unpaid taxes to the exchequer

    (E)   is not the only trouble the hotel could face; it, as well as two other hotels, also owe millions in unpaid taxes to the exchequer

107. As far as acquiring life skills is concerned, <u>learning how to drive is considerably more important than to learn playing the guitar.</u>

    (A)   learning how to drive is considerably more important than to learn playing the guitar

    (B)   learning how to drive is considerably more important than playing the guitar

    (C)   how to drive is considerably more important than how to play the guitar

    (D)   learning to drive is considerably more important than learning to play the guitar

    (E)   to learn driving is considerably more important than to be playing the guitar

108. By the time Tim appears for the GMAT, <u>he will have completed a minimum of eight practice tests, three hundred practice questions, and more than seventy hours spent</u> browsing through the various GMAT forums.

   (A) he will have completed a minimum of eight practice tests, three hundred practice questions, and more than seventy hours spent

   (B) he will complete a minimum of eight practice tests, three hundred practice questions, and he will spend more than seventy hours

   (C) he would have completed a minimum of eight practice tests and three hundred practice questions, spending more than seventy hours

   (D) he would complete a minimum of eight practice tests in addition to completing three hundred practice questions, having spent more than seventy hours

   (E) he will have completed a minimum of eight practice tests and three hundred practice questions, and spent more than seventy hours

109. <u>The consistent rising revenues of the shipping company has convinced analysts that the company is</u> a good one for their clients to invest in.

   (A) The consistent rising revenues of the shipping company has convinced analysts that the company is

   (B) The consistently rising revenues of the shipping company has convinced analysts that the company is

   (C) The consistent rise in the revenues of the shipping company has convinced analysts that the company is

   (D) The consistently rising revenues of the shipping company have convinced analysts that the company was

   (E) The consistent rise in the revenues of the shipping company have convinced analysts that the company is

110. It is indeed ironical to note that the subject <u>where Barry scored the most marks was the one in which he</u> put in the least effort.

   (A) where Barry scored the most marks was the one in which he

   (B) where Barry scored the maximum marks was the same one in which he had

   (C) in which Barry scored the most marks was the one where he

   (D) in which Barry scored the most marks was the one in which he had

   (E) for which Barry scored the highest marks was the one where he

111. An ultrabook is better than a regular laptop because it has a battery that lasts longer, a faster processor, and a sleeker design.

    (A) it has a battery that lasts longer, a faster processor, and a sleeker design

    (B) it has a longer lasting battery, a faster processor, and a design that is sleeker

    (C) of having a battery that lasts longer, a processor that is faster, and a design that is more sleeker

    (D) of the fact that they have longer lasting batteries, faster processors, and a sleeker design

    (E) it has a battery that lasts longer, a processor that is faster, and a design that is sleeker

112. While the term 'sublimation' has several meanings, in scientific terminology it is a process where a substance changes from solid to gaseous state, without entering the liquid state.

    (A) While the term 'sublimation' has several meanings, in scientific terminology it is a process where

    (B) The term 'sublimation' has several meanings, in scientific terminology it is a process in which

    (C) While the term 'sublimation' has several meanings, in scientific terminology it refers to a process in which

    (D) The term 'sublimation' has several meanings, in scientific terminology it refers to a process when

    (E) The term 'sublimation', having several meanings in scientific terminology, refers to a process where

113. The performance of the iron and steel industry this year has been better than that of any other year.

    (A) The performance of the iron and steel industry this year has been better than that of any other year

    (B) The performance of the iron and steel industry this year has been better than in any other year

    (C) The iron and steel industry's performance this year has been better in comparison to any other year

    (D) the iron and steel industry's performance has been better this year than any other year

    (E) This year the performance of the iron and steel industry has been better than that of any other year's performance

114. <u>Raising raw material costs, along with escalating corporate tax rates, has made it very difficult for companies to remain profitable.</u>

(A) Raising raw material costs, along with escalating corporate tax rates, has made it very difficult for companies to remain profitable.

(B) Rising raw material costs and escalating corporate tax rates has made it very difficult for companies to remain profitable.

(C) The rise in raw material costs, along with escalating corporate tax rates, has made it very difficult for companies to remain profitable.

(D) Rising raw material costs, along with escalating corporate tax rates, has made it very difficult for companies to remain profitable

(E) Rising raw material costs, along with escalating corporate tax rates, have made it very difficult for companies to remain profitable.

115. To make <u>figures appear to exist in space on a two-dimensional surface, a few artists in the Renaissance art period developed a system of one point perspective, a mathematical system where all edges and forms</u> follow orthogonal lines converging on a single point.

(A) figures appear to exist in space on a two-dimensional surface, a few artists in the Renaissance art period developed a system of one point perspective, a mathematical system where all edges and forms

(B) figures appear to exist in space, a few artists in the Renaissance art period developed a system of one point perspective on a two-dimensional surface, a mathematical system where all edges and forms

(C) figures on a two-dimensional surface appear to exist in space, a few artists in the Renaissance art period developed a system of one point perspective, a mathematical system in which all edges and forms

(D) figures appear to exist in space on a two-dimensional surface, a few artists in the Renaissance art period developed a system of one point perspective, which is a mathematical system where each edge and form

(E) figures on a two-dimensional surface appear as if they are existing in space, a system of one point perspective was developed by a few artists in the Renaissance art period, a mathematical system where each edge and form

116. Because most investors prefer long term capital gains to annual dividend payouts, <u>the reduction in dividend payout ratios that have taken place during the last decade are</u> perfectly understandable.

(A) the reduction in dividend payout ratios that have taken place during the last decade are

(B) the reduction in dividend payout ratios that has taken place during the last decade is

(C) the reduction that has taken place in dividend payout ratios during the last decade are

(D) the reduction in dividend payout ratios that have taken place during the last decade is

(E) the reduction that has taken place in dividend payout ratios during the last decade is

117. A vocal opponent of the unequal distribution of wealth, the itinerant activist has spent time in several countries across the world, <u>railing against the callousness and injustices of governments, the negligence of the upper classes, and trying to forge a transnational people's movement.</u>

(A) railing against the callousness and injustices of governments, the negligence of the upper classes, and trying to forge a transnational people's movement

(B) to rail against the callousness and injustices of governments and the negligence of the upper classes, and trying to forge a transnational people's movement

(C) railed against the callousness and injustices of governments, the negligence of the upper classes, and tried to forge a transnational people's movement

(D) railing against the callousness and injustices of governments and the negligence of the upper classes, and trying to forge a transnational people's movement

(E) railing against the callousness and injustices of governments, the neglecting of the upper classes, and trying to forge a transnational people's movement

118. Through the last six decades, the missionary group <u>has worked tirelessly for the upliftment of the economically backward sections of the society and have promised that they will continue to do it</u> in future as well.

(A) has worked tirelessly for the upliftment of the economically backward sections of the society and have promised that they will continue to do it

(B) has worked tirelessly for the upliftment of the economically backward sections of the society and has promised that it will continue to do so

(C) has and will continue to work tirelessly for the upliftment of the economically backward sections of the society

(D) has been working tirelessly for the upliftment of the economically backward sections of the society and has promised that they will continue to do it

(E) worked tirelessly for the upliftment of the economically backward sections of the society and have promised that they will continue to do so

119. The State Labour Department has approved <u>an increase in the wages of labourers from other states, a reduction in their tax obligations, and brought</u> joy to the thousands of immigrant labourers living in the city.

   (A)   an increase in the wages of labourers from other states, a reduction in their tax obligations, and brought

   (B)   a wage increase for labourers from other states, reducing their tax obligations, and brought

   (C)   an increase in the wages of labourers from other states and a reduction in their tax obligations, bringing

   (D)   that the wages of labourers from other states be increased and that their tax obligations be reduced, and brought

   (E)   an increase in both the wages of labourers from other states along with a reduction in their tax obligations, bringing

120. <u>Beaten convincingly and fairly by their arch rivals, the city rugby team has promised that they are going to win back the title next year</u>.

   (A)   Beaten convincingly and fairly by their arch rivals, the city rugby team has promised that they are going to win back the title next year

   (B)   Beaten convincingly and fairly by their arch rivals, the city rugby team has promised that it is going to win back the title next year

   (C)   The city rugby team, beaten convincingly and fairly by its arch rival, promised that it will win back the title next year

   (D)   The city rugby team has promised that it would win back the title next year, beaten convincingly and fairly by their arch rivals

   (E)   Beaten convincingly and fairly by its arch rival, the city rugby team has promised that it will win back the title next year

121. <u>Sachin Tendulkar has a style of batting that is different from that of most other players'</u>.

   (A) Sachin Tendulkar has a style of batting that is different from that of most other players'

   (B) Sachin Tendulkar's style of batting that is different than that of most other players

   (C) Sachin Tendulkar has a style of batting that is different than most other players

   (D) Sachin Tendulkar's style of batting is different from that of most other players

   (E) Sachin Tendulkar's batting style that is different from that of most other players.

122. Comparing claimed speeds of the fastest cars in the world, especially in historical cases, is difficult <u>due to there being no standardized method of determining the top speed, nor a central authority to verify any such claims</u>.

    (A)   due to there being no standardized method of determining the top speed, nor a central authority to verify any such claims

    (B)   due to the absence of a standardized method of determining the top speed and a central authority to verify any such claims

    (C)   in that there is neither a standardized method of determining the top speed, nor can such claims be verified by a central authority

    (D)   because of the absence of any standardized method of determining the top speed, and of a central authority to verify any such claims

    (E)   because there is no standardized method of determining the top speed, or of verifying such claims by a central authority

123. The basic process of selecting the President of the United States is spelled out <u>in the U.S. Constitution, which has been modified by subsequent amendments, leading to the addition of many additional steps</u>.

    (A)   in the U.S. Constitution, which has been modified by subsequent amendments, leading to the addition of many additional steps

    (B)   in the U.S. Constitution and it has been modified by subsequent amendments, leading to the addition of many additional steps

    (C)   in the U.S. Constitution and has been modified by subsequent amendments, leading to many additional steps

    (D)   in the U.S. Constitution and is modified by subsequent amendments, which have led to the addition of many additional steps

    (E)   in the U.S. Constitution and has been modified by subsequent amendments, leading to the addition of many steps

124. <u>Each invoice and gate pass must have "PAID" stamped over their number</u>.

    (A)   Each invoice and gate pass must have "PAID" stamped over their number

    (B)   Every one of the invoices and gate passes must have "PAID" stamped over their number

    (C)   Each invoice and gate pass must have "PAID" stamped over its number

    (D)   All invoices and gate passes must have "PAID" stamped over its number

    (E)   Every invoice and each gate pass must have "PAID" stamped over their number

125.   Not only is Dave going to Paris for a month, <u>but also to Rome and then to London for a week each</u>.

     (A)   but also to Rome and then to London for a week each

     (B)   he will also be going to Rome and then to London for a week each

     (C)   but Rome and London too for a week each

     (D)   but he is also going to Rome for a week and then London for a week each

     (E)   but he is also going to Rome and then to London for a week each

Answers & Explanations

Q No.	Ans.	Q No.	Ans.	Q No.	Ans.	Q No.	Ans.	Q No.	Ans.
1	B	26	D	51	D	76	C	101	C
2	A	27	A	52	B	77	E	102	D
3	B	28	D	53	D	78	D	103	D
4	D	29	D	54	C	79	D	104	D
5	C	30	D	55	D	80	D	105	D
6	A	31	C	56	B	81	E	106	C
7	B	32	D	57	D	82	E	107	D
8	D	33	D	58	C	83	C	108	E
9	E	34	E	59	B	84	A	109	C
10	B	35	B	60	A	85	C	110	D
11	C	36	A	61	A	86	E	111	E
12	C	37	D	62	C	87	C	112	C
13	E	38	A	63	C	88	E	113	B
14	D	39	E	64	C	89	C	114	E
15	D	40	A	65	A	90	B	115	C
16	E	41	C	66	B	91	D	116	E
17	D	42	E	67	A	92	E	117	D
18	B	43	E	68	B	93	D	118	B
19	E	44	E	69	C	94	D	119	C
20	E	45	D	70	C	95	D	120	E
21	D	46	D	71	B	96	D	121	D
22	D	47	C	72	A	97	C	122	D
23	C	48	A	73	E	98	A	123	E
24	B	49	D	74	B	99	E	124	C
25	C	50	E	75	E	100	D	125	E

1. **Official Answer (OA) – B**

    Concepts Tested – Usage, Fragment, Modifiers

    A. *Which* incorrectly refers to the *telecommunications industry.*

    B. The correct answer. *Leading* acts as an adverbial modifier modifying the action of the entire previous clause.

    C. *Which* incorrectly refers to *The Bell Company.* This sentence does not contain a main verb; it just has two back to back modifying phrases. The use of the infinitive *to revolutionize* makes it appear as if the purpose of the project is to revolutionize whereas this is just the side effect of the project.

    D. The sentence does not have a main verb; it just contains several back to back modifying phrases and relative clauses

    E. Doesn't look too bad until you realize that the use of *currently* implies the present tense only, so we cannot use the present perfect tense *has been* (which implies that the action started in the past). Also this sentence incorrectly suggests that the new project will do two things – *revolutionize the industry and lower the rates* – whereas the project will just revolutionise the industry and this fact will lower the rates.

2. **Official Answer (OA) – A**

    Concepts Tested – Run on sentences, Meaning

    A. The correct answer

    B. This is a run-on sentence. The conjunctive adverb *however* cannot be used to connect two independent clauses

    C. The uses of *even though* and *yet* in the same sentence is redundant

    D. Distorts the meaning by suggesting that the reason Cristina was able to complete the test in time was because she started later than the rest of the students. This doesn't make any logical sense

    E. Distorts the meaning by reversing the cause and effect relation.

3. **Official Answer (OA) – B**

   Concepts Tested – Comparison, Usage

   A. Makes it appear as though Miroslav Klose was beaten by Ronaldo's goals and not by Ronaldo himself

   B. The correct answer; compares Klose with Ronaldo.

   C. The placement of *only* as an adverb to modify *bettered* is incorrect. *Only* needs to modify *Ronaldo*. Also the sentence makes it appear as though Miroslav Klose was beaten by Ronaldo's goals and not by Ronaldo himself

   D. Incorrectly suggests that Klose was bettered by two things – Ronaldo and his goals

   E. The placement of *only* as an adverb to modify *bettered* is incorrect. *Only* needs to modify Ronaldo. The use of *having* is best avoided on the GMAT

4. **Official Answer (OA) – D**

   Concepts Tested – Subject Verb Agreement, Pronoun case

   A. The plural subject *Priscilla and I* does not agree with the singular verb *was*

   B. The use of the additive phrase *as well as* implies that the subject is only *Priscilla*, and the singular *Priscilla* does not agree with the plural verb *were*. Also *me* is the incorrect pronoun; we require the subject pronoun *I*.

   C. *Me* is the incorrect pronoun; we require the subject pronoun *I*.

   D. The correct answer. The singular *Priscilla* agrees with the singular *was*.

   E. Now it is the *teacher* who is doing the action and *I* am receiving it; hence the pronoun should be the objective *me*.

5. **Official Answer (OA) – C**

    Concepts Tested – Fragment, Parallelism, Tense

    A. This sentence is a fragment because it is missing a main verb such as *decided*. Since *by* comes after *both*, it needs to be repeated before the *general public*

    B. The use of the past perfect tense *had* is incorrect since the sentence does not refer to two past events. Since *by* comes before *both*, it does not need to be repeated before *general public*. The use of *his* in *his extremely graphic violence scenes* is incorrect because the graphic scenes are not of the actor but of the movies.

    C. The correct answer. The placement of *by* is correct and so is the use of tenses.

    D. The sentence talks about two events – *public's criticism and the actor's decision* - that took place at different time periods. First the public criticized and then the actor decided, so the two cannot be in the same time period. This sentence puts both of these in the simple past tense – *were and decided*

    E. There is a verb missing at the end of the sentence giving out the actor's decision. *Deciding* is a participle; the verb would need to be *has decided*

6. **Official Answer (OA) – A**

    Concepts Tested – Subject Verb Agreement, Parallelism

    A. The correct answer. Since the verb *has* comes after *neither*, it needs to be repeated after *nor*.

    B. Since the verb *has* comes after *neither*, it needs to be repeated after *nor*

    C. The plural *plants* does not agree with the singular *has*

    D. The use of *neither of* is incorrect because topsoil and plants are two different things

    E. To get the parallelism correct the part after nor should read – *nor have the plants arrived*

7. **Official Answer (OA) – B**

   Concepts Tested – Modifiers, Idiom

   A. The sentence starts with a modifying phrase so what comes after the comma has to be the person who is the expert i.e. *Edward.*

   B. The correct answer. Gets the modification correct. Also gets the idiom *regarded....as* correct.

   C. The sentence starts with a modifying phrase so what comes after the comma has to be the person who is the expert i.e. *Edward.*

   D. The use of the conjunctive adverb *thus* after the comma is incorrect and makes this a run-on sentence.

   E. Uses the incorrect idiom *considered....to be.*

8. **Official Answer (OA) – D**

   Concepts Tested – Tense, Pronoun Agreement

   A. Unnecessarily uses the present continuous tense (*are ensuring*). This statement applies to all times so should be in the simple present tense. Also the singular noun *passenger* does not agree with the plural pronoun *their.*

   B. The part after the comma contains the pronoun *their*, so the noun has to be the plural *passengers.*

   C. The part after the comma contains the pronoun *their*, so the noun has to be the plural *passengers.*

   D. The correct answer

   E. This sentence is a fragment. There needs to be a helping verb before *ensuring* to use it as a verb.

9. **Official Answer (OA) – E**

   Concepts Tested – Pronoun Reference, Tense

   A. The subject of the sentence is the *ban* so the *it* should ideally refer to the *ban* which doesn't make sense because the government agencies have obviously not stepped up their drive against the ban

   B. The use of the simple past tense *stepped* is incorrect because the action is taking place in the present. Also the use of *it* is ambiguous.

   C. Incorrectly suggests that the government agencies have stepped up their drive against the ban; the agencies have stepped up their drive against plastic bags and not against the ban

   D. The use of *it* is ambiguous

   E. The correct answer

10. **Official Answer (OA) – B**

    Concepts Tested – Parallelism

    A. Since *she* comes before *neither,* it does not have to be repeated after *nor*

    B. The correct answer

    C. The preposition *of* needs to be repeated after *or* to get the parallelism correct

    D. Passive construction is best avoided

    E. Same as D. Also *swimming* and *to surf* are not parallel

11. **Official Answer (OA) – C**

   Concepts Tested – Meaning, Usage, Run on Sentences

   A. This is a run-on sentence because a comma cannot connect two independent clauses

   B. *Which* incorrectly modifies the action of the entire preceding clause

   C. The correct answer. The phrase *a fact* acts as an appositive.

   D. The use of *being* is awkward. Also distorts the meaning by suggesting that London has consciously made its airport one of the busiest in the world.

   E. This sentence again distorts the meaning by suggesting that London has consciously made its airport one of the busiest in the world.

12. **Official Answer (OA) – C**

   Concepts Tested – Modifiers, Meaning

   A. The placement of the phrase *during the felicitation ceremony* makes it appear as if the soldier was tortured during the ceremony itself which is absurd

   B. The relative clause *who had been tortured* should come after *soldier* and not *ceremony*

   C. The correct answer

   D. Distorts the meaning by suggesting that the soldier's mother was tortured

   E. The *his* is ambiguous as we don't know whether it refers to the soldier or to the war veteran. The use of the appositive *a soldier* after the comma would only be correct if the earlier clause were to end with *soldier* which it does not.

13. **Official Answer (OA) – E**

   Concepts Tested – Pronoun reference

   A. Since the subject of the clause before the comma is *polarised sunglasses*, these should, to maintain parallelism, ideally be the subject of the clause after the comma as well. You cannot use *these* on its own; it needs to be followed by *glasses*. The use of *their* is ambiguous.

   B. The use of too many *their's* is ambiguous and awkward. Also the singular *coating* does not agree with the plural *make*.

   C. The singular pronoun *it* cannot refer to the plural *sunglasses*.

   D. The phrase *because of the coating on these glasses* is awkward and wordy. Also the infinitive *to read* is preferred to the gerund *reading*.

   E. The correct answer.

14. **Official Answer (OA) – D**

   Concepts Tested – Tense

   This sentence is testing you on your understanding of time periods. The non underlined part states that *as people become something*. When will this happen? Obviously in the future. So the effect – demand for mineral water – will also take place in the future.

   A. Incorrectly uses the present continuous tense (*is increasing*) instead of the future tense.

   B. Incorrectly uses the present perfect continuous tense (*has been increasing*) instead of the future tense. Also the sentence incorrectly makes *providing* parallel with *assuring*. *Providing* in fact is common to both the benefits of bottled water and hence should ideally be placed before *both*.

   C. Incorrectly uses the present perfect tense (*has increased*) instead of the future tense. The use of *assures* as a verb is incorrect because *provides* has already been used earlier.

   D. The correct answer

   E. Incorrectly uses the simple present tense (*increases*) instead of the future tense. Incorrectly makes *providing* and *assuring* parallel.

15. **Official Answer (OA) – D**

     Concepts Tested – Parallelism, Subject Verb Agreement

     A. The plural *rules* does not agree with the singular *does* or with the singular *it*.

     B. The clauses before and after *not* are not parallel

     C. The use of *nor* along with *not* is incorrect because the subject is not repeating after nor. In this case you need to use *or* instead of *nor*

     D. The correct answer

     E. Wordy. Also the plural *rules* does not agree with the singular *allows*.

16. **Official Answer (OA) – E**

     Concepts Tested – Modifiers, Meaning

     A. The sentence is comparing the male and female birds of one particular species saying that the male is smaller and has red markings over its feathers. This option makes it appear (because of the use and placement of *having*) as if the male is smaller than the particular female that has red markings over its feathers.

     B. Same problem as A. Also *as small as* is different from *smaller*

     C. The use of *that* removes the main verb *is* from the sentence turning it into a fragment

     D. The use of *with* does not parallel the verb *is*. Also you do not require the *is* after *female*.

     E. The correct answer. The use of comma after *female* turns the last clause into an adverbial modifier that modifies the action of the entire preceding clause.

17. **Official Answer (OA) – D**

   Concepts Tested – Subject Verb Agreement

   A. Requires the singular pronoun *its* to refer to *company* and the singular verb *was*

   B. Requires the singular verb *was*

   C. Since there are two orders, the correct term is *orders* and not *order*

   D. The correct answer

   E. Awkward and ungrammatical construction

18. **Official Answer (OA) – B**

   Concepts Tested – Usage, Idiom

   A. *Where* is used to refer only to places and can't be used to refer to subjects; use *in which* instead. Also the adjective *poor* needs to be the adverb *poorly* (modifying the verb *performed*)

   B. The correct answer

   C. The correct idiom is *both......and*. The adjective *poor* needs to be the adverb *poorly* (modifying the verb *performed*)

   D. The use of *being* is awkward and since there is a better option in B, go with B instead. Also the use of *where* is incorrect

   E. Same as A

19. **Official Answer (OA) – E**

   Concepts Tested – Run-on sentences

   A. The use of a comma to connect two independent clauses leads to a run-on sentence.

   B. Same as A.

   C. Looks correct but notice that it talks about *overseas corporates* and so is a distortion of the meaning of the sentence.

   D. This sentence has no meaning because there is no connection between the *United States* and *relaxation* unless the *United States* had an apostrophe at the end (United States)

   E. The correct answer.

20. **Official Answer (OA) – E**

   Concepts Tested – Modifiers, Meaning, Tense

   A. Looks fine until you notice the phrase *over the last one and a half decades*. This suggests that the action comes up to the present (the use of *things have got harder* is a big clue for you), necessitating the use of the Present perfect tense and not the simple past tense (*ceased, felt*)

   B. Uses two back to back modifying phrases at the beginning. There is no verb in the clause before *but*.

   C. The opening phrase makes it appear as if the robust economy had the *well educated citizens. However* needs to be preceded by a semi colon.

   D. The modifying phrase (*with a robust economy and well educated and well to do citizens*) is ambiguously placed because we don't know whether it is referring to Zimbabwe or to South Africa. The use of *it* is also ambiguous.

   E. The correct answer.

21. **Official Answer (OA) – D**

    Concepts Tested – Tense

    A. The use of the simple past tense *reached* is incorrect; we require the past perfect tense *(had reached)* because the sentence actually talks about two different time periods in the past. Notice that Sam *did* not get to holiday in Germany. This is the latter event in the past and so uses the simple past tense *did*. It was obviously before this that Sam could not reach the airport, making this the earlier event in the past and necessitating the use of the past perfect tense *had*.

    B. The construction does not make sense with the rest of the sentence

    C. Same as B

    D. The correct answer.

    E. Again this construction has no meaning.

22. **Official Answer (OA) – D**

    Concepts Tested – Tense, Usage

    A. The use of past perfect tense *had* is incorrect. *Did so* is always preferred to *did it*

    B. *Did so* is always preferred to *did it*

    C. *Tell* is the incorrect tense; you need the simple past tense *told* to match the tense used in the rest of the sentence

    D. The correct answer

    E. *Believes* is the incorrect tense; you need the simple past tense *believed* to match the tense used in the rest of the sentence

23. **Official Answer (OA) – C**

   Concepts Tested – Usage

   A. *Which* cannot be used to modify the action of the entire preceding clause

   B. This is a run-on sentence because the part after the comma is an independent clause

   C. The correct answer

   D. The inverted construction makes this sentence very awkward and unclear

   E. Wordy. C conveys the same meaning more crisply.

24. **Official Answer (OA) – B**

   Concepts Tested – Parallelism

   A. Since *from* comes before *either*, you don't require *as a result of* after *or*

   B. The correct answer

   C. By removing *it is*, the sentence becomes a fragment because there is no main verb in the sentence

   D. Same as C

   E. By removing the other *policies* from the sentence, the comparison gets distorted. Also to maintain parallelism you need to repeat *on* after *rather than*

25. **Official Answer (OA) – C**

Concepts Tested – Idiom, Parallelism

    A. The correct idiom is *prefer...to*

    B. *Hold cash* is not parallel to *investing in property*

    C. The correct answer

    D. Unnecessarily uses the present continuous tense (*are preferring*). The correct idiom is *prefer...to*

    E. The use of *rather* and *prefer* together is redundant since they are both used to show preference.

26. **Official Answer (OA) – D**

Concepts Tested – Subject verb Agreement

    A. The plural subject *factors* does not agree with the singular verb *seems*

    B. The use of the non restrictive *which* is incorrect since we are talking about some specific factors and not about factors in general

    C. The phrase *indicate an economy* has no meaning. You require a *that* after *indicate*

    D. The correct answer

    E. The use of the non restrictive *which* is incorrect since we are talking about some specific factors and not about factors in general. The plural subject *factors* does not agree with the singular verb *seems*

27. **Official Answer (OA) – A**

Concepts Tested – Modifiers, Meaning, Usage

A. The sentence is correct. The adverbial modifier *stating* correctly modifies the action of the entire previous clause. Also the placement of *only* to modify *staff members* is correct

B. The use of the verb *stated* is incorrect as the verb (*has decided*) has already come earlier in the sentence. The placement of *only* to modify *given* is incorrect

C. The use of *by* creates a causal chain not implied by the actual sentence (in which case the comma shouldn't have been used after *staff*). The use of *only* to modify *bonuses* is incorrect and so is the use of *that* to modify *staff members*

D. The placement of *only* is incorrect as it distorts the meaning of the sentence

E. Since the sentence is in the present tense the use of *would* is incorrect.

28. **Official Answer (OA) – D**

Concepts Tested – Parallelism, Pronoun Agreement, Subject Verb Agreement

A. The correct phrase will be *neither of these activities **is** by **itself***. Also *use* needs to come after *either* so that it can parallel *make* after *or*.

B. The correct phrase will be *neither of these activities **is** by **itself***

C. *Land use changes have to be made* is passive and breaks the parallelism. *Themselves* needs to be *itself*.

D. The correct answer

E. There is no need to repeat the pronoun *it* after *or* as this breaks the parallelism

29. **Official Answer (OA) – D**

   Concepts Tested – Usage, Idioms

   A.   *More better* is a redundant phrase. Also *better* needs to be followed by *than*.

   B.   *Much better* needs to be followed by *than*, it cannot be much better *as*

   C.   *As better* needs to be followed by *as* and not by *than*

   D.   The correct answer

   E.   *More better* is a redundant phrase.

30. **Official Answer (OA) – D**

   Concepts Tested – Subjunctive Mood, Idiom

   A.   Since the sentence talks about a hypothetical situation, it requires the use of the subjunctive mood. The use of *if* should have given you a clue to the same. The subjunctive mood requires the use of *would* and *were*. The use of *was* will be incorrect. Also *declare....as* is the incorrect idiom, the correct idiom is only *declare*

   B.   *Declare....as* is the incorrect idiom, the correct idiom is only *declare*

   C.   The use of *was* is incorrect; we require *were* instead

   D.   The correct answer

   E.   Same as C.

31. **Official Answer (OA) – C**

   Concepts Tested – Usage, Comparison

   A. The use of *less* to modify *the number of paintings* (a countable noun) is incorrect; use *fewer* instead. Also the sentence incorrectly compares paintings made this year with last year. The use of *do so* is preferred to *do it*.

   B. The use of *smaller* distorts the meaning of the sentence. Also the phrase *did last year* makes it appear as if last year did something on its own (the correct phrase should be *than he did last year*). The use of *do so* is preferred to *do it*.

   C. The correct answer

   D. The use of *lesser* to modify the *number of paintings* (a countable noun) is incorrect. Also the use of *was done* doesn't make sense because paintings cannot be *done* and in any case there must have been more than one painting.

   E. The use of *do so* is preferred to *do it* because *it* can only be used to refer to a noun.

32. **Official Answer (OA) – D**

   Concepts Tested – Parallelism, Modifier, Meaning

   A. The sentence is ambiguous and does not make it clear who is organizing the training sessions. Also if the Club did two things then they should be parallel – *purchased and organized*

   B. The use of *for them* in the last item in the list breaks the parallel structure in the sentence.

   C. The use of *additionally* is awkward and the use of *professionally* as an adverb distorts the intended meaning of the term.

   D. The correct answer

   E. The last part - *both leading as well as professional golfers* – makes it appear as though the training sessions were with two different categories of golfers.

33. **Official Answer (OA) – D**

Concepts Tested – Tense

A. This sentence is all about consistency. *Mandy's expectations* have to be in an earlier time period than the *Board's response*. So while A looks good, it is incorrect because it places both the actions in the same time period (*did, was expecting*). The expectation will have to be in the past perfect tense for this to be correct.

B. Tense mismatch. The *expectation* is in the simple past tense (*was*) and the *response* is in the past perfect tense (*had not surprised*). It should actually be the other way around.

C. Tense mismatch. This option puts both the actions in the past perfect tense.

D. The correct answer. The earlier action *expectation* is in the past perfect tense (*had expected*) and the latter action *response* is in the simple past tense (*did not surprise*)

E. The use of a semi colon and a conjunction (*because*) together is incorrect. Also the tense is mismatched because both the events are in the simple past tense.

34. **Official Answer (OA) – E**

Concepts Tested – Comparison, Usage

A. The *number of students in class today* cannot be compared with *yesterday*. The *number* should also be *lower* and not *smaller*. Again the *number* cannot be lower than *last week*.

B. The use of past perfect *had been* is not required because the sentence does not talk about two events in the past. Also the *number* cannot be lower than *last week* but *last week's number*.

C. The use of *much* to modify the countable *students* is incorrect. Also the *number of students in class today* cannot be compared with *yesterday*

D. The omission of *more* removes the comparison implied in the sentence. Also the use of *less* is incorrect; it should be *lower*.

E. The correct answer

35. **Official Answer (OA) – B**

Concepts Tested – Modifiers

    A. The sentence starts with a long modifying phrase so whoever is doing all those activities needs to come after the comma i.e. *Lawrence*. Hence A is incorrect.

    B. The correct answer

    C. Same as A.

    D. Same as A.

    E. The use of the past perfect tense *had* is incorrect because the sentence does not mention two different past events.

36. **Official Answer (OA) – A**

Concepts Tested – Parallelism

    A. While *funded* and *looking* may not appear parallel at first glance, note that these are not used as verbs but as adjectives (participles) to modify the *start-up company*. Hence the construction is absolutely correct because a past participle can easily parallel a present participle.

    B. The participle *funded* can not parallel the verb *looked*.

    C. The phrase *funding by a group of angel investors* has no meaning because the gerund *funding* cannot parallel the participle *looking*.

    D. The singular *group* does not agree with the plural verb *have*. Also this sentence completely distorts the meaning of the original sentence by suggesting that the funding was to make use of its first mover advantage.

    E. The use of *having been* is awkward. The plural pronoun *their* cannot refer to the singular company.

37. **Official Answer (OA) – D**

   Concepts Tested – Tense, Usage

   A. *For stopping* is unidiomatic, the correct usage is *to stop*.

   B. The past perfect tense is not required since the sentence does not talk about two past events at different times

   C. The plural *Dikes* does not agree with the singular *has*

   D. The correct answer

   E. Same as B

38. **Official Answer (OA) – A**

   Concepts Tested – Subject Verb Agreement, Idioms

   A. The correct answer. Plural subject *countries* agrees with the plural verb *have,* and the correct idiom is *sanctions on*

   B. Singular *has* does not agree with plural *countries*. The correct idiom is *sanctions on*

   C. The use of *which* is incorrect

   D. The use of *which* is incorrect

   E. The correct idiom is *sanctions on*

39. **Official Answer (OA) – E**

   Concepts Tested – Subject Verb Agreement, Usage

   A. The subject is plural *employees* which does not agree with the singular *has*.

   B. The subject is plural *employees* which does not agree with the singular *has*.

   C. The subject is plural *employees* which does not agree with the singular *has*.

   D. The usage of *which* is incorrect. The phrase *for the benefit of* is wordy

   E. The correct answer

40. **Official Answer (OA) – A**

   Concepts Tested – Meaning, Modifiers

   A. The correct answer

   B. This looks fine until you realise that the subject of this sentence is the *gearbox* and not the *car*. So this sentence essentially says that the gearbox can reach a speed of 125 mph which is absurd.

   C. This sentence does not have a main verb such as *reaches*

   D. Same as B

   E. The use of *which* to modify the action of the entire preceding clause is incorrect.

41. **Official Answer (OA) – C**

   Concepts Tested – Modifiers

   A. The sentence starts with a modifying phrase so what follows should be the *government*. Also *that* should be closer to *measures*

   B. The sentence starts with a modifying phrase so what follows should be the *government*. The use of *which* is incorrect

   C. The correct answer

   D. The part before the comma is incomplete as the government must have used the pretext to do something but this clause never clarifies this. *Proposing* needs to be used as a verb as this is the action that the government took.

   E. The sentence starts with a modifying phrase so what follows should be the *government*.

42. **Official Answer (OA) – E**

   Concepts Tested – Parallelism, Usage

   A. The use of *not as* necessitates the use of *but as*

   B. The semi colon is not needed because the part after the comma is an appositive phrase

   C. Since *as* comes before *not*, it does not need to be repeated after *but*

   D. The use of the phrase *an obvious fact* distorts the meaning of the sentence

   E. The correct sentence

43. Official Answer (OA) – E

Concepts Tested – Modifiers, Subjunctive

A. The modifying phrase *during the course of one's preparation for the GMAT* needs to be followed by whoever is preparing for the GMAT i.e. *One.*

B. Same as A

C. The modifying phrase comes at the end and far away from the subject *one.*

D. Same as A

E. The correct answer

44. Official Answer (OA) – E

Concepts Tested – Wordiness, Tense

A. The use of *at least* and *more* in the same sentence is redundant.

B. The use of *at least* and *more* in the same sentence is redundant.

C. Unnecessarily adds the pronoun *it.* The use of *at least* and *more* in the same sentence is redundant.

D. There is a difference between *as many as* and *at least,* so this option distorts the meaning of the original sentence. However this may not be enough to eliminate this choice as sometimes the original meaning can itself be incorrect. In that case notice that this belief is still true (*believed to have been*) so the use of past tense were is incorrect.

E. The correct answer.

45. Official Answer (OA) – D

Concepts Tested – Parallelism, Idiom

A. *Not just* or *not only* always requires *but also.*

B. Since the preposition *on* comes after *not just,* a suitable preposition (*in*) needs to come after *but also*

C. Since the preposition *on* comes before *not just,* it is assumed that it also applies to whatever comes after *but also* i.e. boardrooms, but *on* is not the correct preposition to refer to boardrooms; we should instead use *in*

D. The correct answer.

E. The use of the preposition *for* is incorrect because *Fortune…..brave* is a mantra for the fighter who is fighting *on* the battlefield. It is not the battlefield itself that is doing the fighting.

46. Official Answer (OA) – D

Concepts Tested – Meaning, Pronoun Reference

A. This looks correct but notice that *he* does not have an antecedent in the sentence. *He* cannot refer to the possessive *student's indifference*

B. The passive construction is awkward.

C. Same as B.

D. The correct answer. Corrects the problem in option A by inserting the noun *student*

E. Same as A. Also the idiomatic construction is *attempt to attend* and not *attempt for attending*

47. **Official Answer (OA) – C**

   Concepts Tested – Usage, Idiom

   A. You cannot use *like* to give examples. The correct idiom is *considered* and not *considered to be*

   B. The correct idiom is *considered* and not *considered to be*

   C. The correct answer

   D. The use of *such....like* is incorrect. The main verb *are* is also missing.

   E. This sentence is a fragment because the main verb *are* is missing.

48. **Official Answer (OA) – A**

   Concepts Tested – Usage, Comparison

   A. The correct answer.

   B. This option gets the comparison wrong. Since *unlike* is followed by his other acquisitions, the part after the comma should also mention an acquisition and not Zuckerberg.

   C. Awkward construction. Also doesn't specify that the other acquisitions were absorbed by Facebook

   D. The correct future tense is *will* and not *is to be*

   E. The phrase *quickly absorbed into Facebook* is unclear. The part after the comma needs to start with either a relative pronoun or another acquisition. Also *will be running independently* does not clarify Zuckerberg's intentions.

49. **Official Answer (OA) – D**

   Concepts Tested – Modifier

   A. It's confusing how many things the new engine offers – if it's two things (*reduction and improvements*) then we need an *and* before *improvements*. If it is three things (*reduction, improvements, environmental emissions*) then *environmental emissions* is not parallel to the other two items.

   B. Same as A

   C. This option correctly uses *and* before *improvements*. However, we require another *and* before *has* because the sentence as a whole is telling us two things about the aircraft engine – that it provides the two features (reduction and improvement) *and* that it has been hailed by the aviation industry.

   D. The correct answer

   E. Very awkward and confusing construction. D is much more concise and clear.

50. **Official Answer (OA) – E**

   Concepts Tested – Tense

   A. The use of *since* to refer to a duration (eight months) is incorrect.

   B. The use of *having been driving* is awkward and unnecessary. The use of *it* is ambiguous as it appears as though *it* is referring to *the clutch* and not to *the car*

   C. The use of *since* to refer to a duration (eight months) is incorrect. The use of the present continuous tense (*is still finding*) is best avoided.

   D. The use of *since* to refer to a duration (eight months) is incorrect. The use of *it* is ambiguous as it appears as though *it* is referring to the clutch and not to the car

   E. The correct answer. Correctly uses *for* to refer to a duration. Also replaces the ambiguous *it* with the car.

51. **Official Answer (OA) – D**

   Concepts Tested –Subject Verb Agreement, Idioms

   A. The plural *counterparts* does not agree with the singular *tends*. The *or* should actually be *nor*.

   B. The use of *more* requires *than* and not *as*. The use of *being* is awkward.

   C. The use of *more* requires *than* and not *as*. The *or* should actually be *nor*.

   D. The correct answer

   E. *As nutritious than* is the incorrect idiom, it should be *as nutritious as*. The phrase *also not likely to be* is awkward in context of the sentence

52. **Official Answer (OA) – B**

   Concepts Tested – Parallelism

   A. *Collecting* and *expose* are not parallel. While *where* looks correct by itself, if you read the entire non underlined part – *where sodium chloride or common salt finally crystallizes at the bottom of the ponds* – it doesn't make sense to say *where* when you are again stating *at the bottom of the ponds*. This actually creates ambiguity.

   B. The correct answer

   C. *Collecting* and *expose* are not parallel. *Which* incorrectly refers to the *sun*. The use of *where* is incorrect.

   D. The phrase *exposing some sea water in a pond to the sun* is very awkward and confusing.

   E. Unnecessarily makes *start* and *collect* parallel. The use of *it* after *then* makes it ambiguous as *it* could also refer to the *pond*. The phrase *from which* is also incorrect because the salt doesn't crystallize from the harvesting ponds but after this process is over.

53. Official Answer (OA) – D

Concepts Tested – Modifiers, Usage

A. The use of *if* to state alternatives is incorrect, use *whether* instead.

B. The two things Lewis is confused between are not parallel. Also the correct idiom is *between....and*

C. The sentence starts with a modifying phrase so what comes after the comma has to be *Lewis*. The use of *if* to state alternatives is incorrect, use *whether* instead.

D. The correct answer

E. The sentence starts with a modifying phrase so what comes after the comma has to be *Lewis*.

54. Official Answer (OA) – C

Concepts Tested – Comparison, Meaning

A. To get this right, it is very important to understand the meaning implied by the original sentence. The sentence basically states that the price of a house depends more on its location than on its quality of construction. Obviously A is then incorrect because it correlates the location with the quality of construction whereas both of these factors have to actually correlate with the price.

B. The use of *more* necessitates the use of *than* and not *as*

C. The correct answer. It basically states that the location correlates more with the price than does the quality (correlate with the price)

D. Incorrectly correlates the location with the quality of construction. Also the correct idiom is *correlate with*.

E. The correct idiom is *correlate with*. Also this sentence has the same meaning problem as did option A

55. **Official Answer (OA) – D**

Concepts Tested – Subjunctive Mood, Usage

A. The use of the verb *recommends* tells us that the sentence needs to be in the subjunctive mood. The use of *he* is incorrect because *he* can't refer to the possessive *Robert's*. Also the use of *should* with *recommend* is redundant.

B. The use of *should* with *recommend* is redundant

C. You do not use *will* with the subjunctive mood.

D. The correct answer

E. You do not use the infinitive *to be* with the subjunctive mood, you only use the *be*.

56. **Official Answer (OA) – B**

Concepts Tested – Idiom, Parallelism

A. The correct idiom is *between.....and*

B. The correct answer. *Quitting* and *continuing* are also parallel

C. The correct idiom is *between.....and*

D. The correct idiom is *between.....and*

E. The use of *whether* is not required. *To continue* is not parallel to *quitting*

57. **Official Answer (OA) – D**

   Concepts Tested – Parallelism, Idiom

   A. *To be a good individual* is not parallel to *being successful*

   B. The use of *more* requires the use of *than* and not *in comparison to*

   C. Same as B

   D. The correct answer. Don't assume that *being* will always be incorrect.

   E. Wordy and awkward construction. D is more concise.

58. **Official Answer (OA) – C**

   Concepts Tested – Subjunctive Mood

   A. The use of *suggested* should tell you that the subjunctive mood will be required in this sentence. So *avoids* needs to be *avoid* and the verb *is* after bandage needs to be *be*

   B. The subjunctive mood never uses the infinitive *to avoid*. Also the use of *suggest* and *should* in the same sentence is redundant.

   C. The correct answer

   D. The use of *suggest* and *should* in the same sentence is redundant

   E. The subjunctive mood never uses the infinitive *to avoid*

59. **Official Answer (OA) – B**

Concepts Tested – Parallelism

   A. The three things in the list – *losing, improving, to widen* – are not parallel

   B. The correct answer

   C. Either use *for* only with the first item in the series or use it with all the three items.

   D. All the items in the series need to be preceded by a preposition such as *for* because Americans are visiting gyms *for* losing weight or *to* lose weight

   E. Either use *to* only with the first item in the series or use it with all the three items.

60. **Official Answer (OA) – A**

Concepts Tested – Usage, Comparison, Pronoun Agreement

   A. The correct answer. While you may think that *which* is referring to *Chetan Bhagat*, it is actually referring to *books*. Sometimes a necessary modifier can come in between *which* and the noun it modifies. The plural verb *are* should also give you a clue that the subject is *books*. And finally there is no better option than this, so you go with A.

   B. The singular *that* cannot refer to plural *books*. Also there needs to be *other* before *Indian writer*.

   C. The use of the restrictive *that* is incorrect because even if we assume that *that* is referring to *books* and not to *Chetan Bhagat*, the use of the restrictive modifier itself is incorrect since the sentence is talking about all of Chetan Bhagat's books and not a few specific ones. Also there needs to be *other* before Indian writer.

   D. This sentence is a fragment since the main verb *are* is missing

   E. Incorrectly compares *Indian writers* with the *books of Chetan Bhagat*.

61. **Official Answer (OA) – A**

Concepts Tested – Tense, Subject Verb Agreement

    A. This sentence is correct because the cause (*soaring demand*) and the effect (*reel under losses*) are both in the same tense.

    B. *Demand* cannot *soar* but *soars*. Also if the first clause (which is the cause) is in the simple present tense, the second clause (which is the effect) cannot be in the present perfect continuous tense.

    C. If the first clause (which is the cause) is in the present perfect tense, the second clause (which is the effect) cannot be in the simple past tense.

    D. If the first clause (which is the cause) is in the simple present tense, the second clause (which is the effect) cannot be in the present perfect tense.

    E. Wordy and awkward. The verb *are* is missing from in front of *reeling*

62. **Official Answer (OA) – C**

Concepts Tested – Parallelism, Run on Sentences, Subject Verb Agreement

    A. The use of a comma to connect two independent clauses is incorrect. Also what greeted the minister *were* (and not *was*) three things

    B. The use of *and* fails to demonstrate the contrast inherent in the two clauses. Also *the minister's expectations* need to be in the past perfect tense because the *expectations* were there before the *greeting* (which is in the simple past tense greeted)

    C. The correct answer

    D. *However* needs to be preceded by a semi colon when it is used to connect two independent clauses. Also what greeted the minister *were* (and not *was*) three things

    E. This is a fragment because the helping verb (*was, had been, etc.*) is missing from before *expecting*

63. **Official Answer (OA) – C**

   Concepts Tested – Modifiers, Parallelism

   A.   The use of *their* is ambiguous because it can refer to *strategies* or *insights*.

   B.   Since the sentence starts with a modifying phrase, what follows the comma should be the *company* and not its *plan*

   C.   The correct answer

   D.   The phrase *looking at applying* is awkward and unidiomatic. Also the placement of *using local insights* after the comma incorrectly implies that it applies to both – *applying and expanding*.

   E.   Same as B

64. **Official Answer (OA) – C**

   Concepts Tested – Wordiness, Meaning

   A.   The use of the restrictive modifier *that* is incorrect since there is only one *Iran* in the world and this fact – *that it has the world's fourth-largest oil reserves* – applies to all of *Iran*. So the non restrictive modifier *which* should be used instead.

   B.   The use of *having* is awkward and unidiomatic

   C.   The correct answer

   D.   Wordy. C states the same thing more concisely

   E.   Wordy again and it's best to avoid pronouns such as *its* in the correct answer.

65. **Official Answer (OA) – A**

Concepts Tested – Tense, Usage, Idiom

A. The correct answer.

B. The use of *them* is incorrect as it creates an independent clause leading to a distortion of meaning. The use of *if* to evaluate alternatives is incorrect. The correct idiom is *worry about*

C. The use of *who* restricts the officials to only those who equate patriotism with supporting the government's policies. Also we require the simple past tense *began* and not the participle *begun*. The use of *if* to evaluate alternatives is incorrect. The correct idiom is *worry about*

D. *Which* cannot be used to refer to *officials*. The use of *begun* is incorrect. The correct idiom is *worry about*

E. We require the simple past tense *began* and not the participle *begun*. The correct idiom is *worry about*

66. **Official Answer (OA) – B**

Concepts Tested – Comparison

A. While it may appear that this sentence is testing you on the use of *equivalent/equal/same* this is not the case (and will rarely ever be the case). This sentence is actually testing you on comparison of logical items. This sentence compares the *rise in the level of pollutants* with the *level of pollutants* (and not with the *rise*), so is incorrect.

B. The correct answer. *That* refers back to *rise*

C. This option erroneously compares *rise* with the *level of pollutants* in Ohio River

D. While *that* can refer back to *rise*, we still need to mention what this *rise* has been in

E. Same as D

67. **Official Answer (OA) – A**

   Concepts Tested – Meaning

   A. The correct answer

   B. This option makes the part after the underline appear disconnected from the rest of the sentence. Also the use of comma before the verb *are* is incorrect.

   C. The placement of *both* distorts the meaning of the sentence because there are no two things coming after *both*.

   D. The use of *being* is awkward. *Cultural reference frame* is different from *cultural frame of reference* since it could very well refer to a particular type of frame.

   E. The use of the verb *have* after the comma is incorrect. Also the part after the underline appears disconnected from the rest of the sentence.

68. **Official Answer (OA) – B**

   Concepts Tested – Idiom

   A. The correct idiom is *considered* and not *considered to be*.

   B. The correct answer

   C. The correct idiom is *regarded....as*. The phrase *relegating it...* doesn't make it clear who or what is doing the relegation

   D. The past perfect tense (*had been*) is not required because the sentence only talks about one event in the past.

   E. The correct idiom is *considered* and not *considered as. Which* incorrectly refers to *trade*.

69. **Official Answer (OA) – C**

   Concepts Tested – Modifier

   A. The sentence starts with a modifying phrase so whoever is doing the detection needs to come after the comma i.e. *one*.

   B. Same as A

   C. The correct answer.

   D. *Be aware* in C is more concise than *have awareness of* in Dwhich is wordy and awkward.

   E. Same as A

70. **Official Answer (OA) – C**

   Concepts Tested – Idiom

   A. *Belief.... about* is unidiomatic; a better construction is *belief.... that*. The use of *being* is best avoided.

   B. Same as A.

   C. The correct answer

   D. Same as A. Also the placement of the phrase *in some cultures* is ambiguous.

   E. Awkward and unclear construction

71. **Official Answer (OA) – B**

   Concepts Tested – Parallelism, Modifiers

   A. The opening phrase tells us two things about the Suez Canal – it was constructed by XYZ and it is connecting A to B. The use of *connected* would obviously be incorrect since it is acting as a verb and we require an adjective (participle). Also the opening phrase needs to be followed by the *Suez canal*.

   B. The correct answer.

   C. *Having been* is awkward and unidiomatic. B conveys the same meaning more clearly

   D. This sentence makes it appear as if the *Suez Canal Company* was connecting the two seas.

   E. The use of the past perfect tense *had been* is incorrect since the sentence does not talk about two different events in the past.

72. **Official Answer (OA) – A**

   Concepts Tested – Subject Verb Agreement

   A. Since the subject is plural (because of the use of and), the verb cannot be the singular *is*.

   B. The use of plural *are* does not agree with the singular *characteristic*

   C. The use of the additive phrase *as well as* suggests that the verb needs to be the singular *is* to match the singular subject phrase *absence of an atmosphere*.

   D. The use of plural *are* does not agree with the singular *characteristic*

   E. The correct answer

73. **Official Answer (OA) – E**

   Concepts Tested – Modifiers, Subject Verb Agreement, Parallelism

   A. We need the adverb *seemingly* to modify the adjective *unlimited*. The plural subject (because of the use of *and*) does not agree with the singular verb *makes*.

   B. We need the adverb *seemingly* to modify the adjective *unlimited*.

   C. Same as B. Also we require the adverb *apparently* to modify the adjective *absent*

   D. Since the first clause has a prepositional phrase (*of fresh water*), the second clause should also have a prepositional phrase to maintain parallelism. Also the plural subject does not agree with the singular verb *makes*

   E. The correct answer. Both the clauses make use of prepositional phrases.

74. **Official Answer (OA) – B**

   Concepts Tested – Parallelism, Idiom

   A. The purpose of the driving test is to asses a person's ability of doing two things – *recognizing traffic signs and steering and controlling a vehicle*. These two need to be parallel. *Of recognizing* and *to steer* are obviously not parallel. The idiomatic construction is *ability to do* something

   B. The correct answer

   C. Looks a little wordy but correct. However notice that the non underlined part says *and control*; *steering* is obviously not parallel to this.

   D. The purpose of something is *to* do something, so the use of *for assessing* is unidiomatic.

   E. Unnecessarily wordy. The use of *of* in the phrase *of his ability for steering* does not make sense. Also *steering* is not parallel to *control*.

75. **Official Answer (OA) – E**

   Concepts Tested – Subjunctive Mood, Meaning

   A. In the subjunctive mood, verbs such as *mandate* always need to be followed by *that*. Also the use of *to be* in the subjunctive mood is incorrect; you only use *be*.

   B. The use of *mandated* and *should* in the same sentence creates an oxymoron. *Mandate* is an order and *should* implies suggestion, so they both can't exist together.

   C. This sentence has no meaning as it eliminates *that*. The last part *for their children provided access* also doesn't make any sense

   D. *That* needs to come immediately after *mandated*. The use of *will* is incorrect since the sentence is in the subjunctive mood.

   E. The correct answer.

76. **Official Answer (OA) – C**

   Concepts Tested – Parallelism, Usage

   A. The usage of *due to* is incorrect

   B. Since *more* is followed by *by*, parallelism requires that *than* also be followed by *by* and not *due to*

   C. The correct answer; both the clauses start with *because of*

   D. The usage of *due to* is incorrect. Also *due to* and *because of* are not parallel

   E. Passive and awkward construction. Also does not maintain parallelism

77. **Official Answer (OA) – E**

Concepts Tested – Subject Verb Agreement, Run on Sentence

    A. The singular *each* does not agree with the plural *specialise*

    B. In this case the subject is the plural *divisions* which does not agree with the singular *specialises*

    C. This is a run-on sentence since the part after the comma is an independent clause

    D. This is a run-on sentence as well

    E. The correct answer

78. **Official Answer (OA) – D**

Concepts Tested – Parallelism, Pronoun Reference

    A. The clause after *but* is unnecessarily wordy and awkward. The use of multiple *it's* further complicates things.

    B. The use of the verb *is* after the comma doesn't make sense. The rest of the sentence is equally awkward and ungrammatical

    C. The use of *being* makes this sentence awkward as does the clause after *but*. Also the use of *that* to refer to *people* is incorrect.

    D. The correct answer. No pronoun is needed after *but* because the sentence has just one subject – *differential pricing of gasoline*.

    E. The use of *them* is incorrect. The main verb is missing from in front of often (*has been*)

79. **Official Answer (OA) – D**

Concepts Tested – Modifiers, Comparison

A.   The opening clause is trying to make two things equal – *the delight* of the shareholder and *the distress* of the competitors. The use of the phrase *as much as* necessitates the use of the noun *move* before both the things being compared; repeating the noun *move* becomes awkward so we need a *it* before distressed to get the comparison correct - the *move* delighted the shareholders as much as *it* (the move) distressed the competitors. Also the use of *and* is incorrect because it is not connecting two independent thoughts; rather one is the cause of the other.

B.   Since the sentence starts with a modifying phrase, what follows the comma should be the two shipping companies.

C.   The phrase *move delighting their shareholders* is awkward and unclear. Also as discussed in A, *it* needs to be inserted after *as much as*. The use of *which* is also incorrect because *which* cannot modify the action of the entire preceding clause.

D.   The correct answer. Correctly uses the adverbial modifier *leading* to modify the action of the entire preceding clause.

E.   This sentence suggests that the two shipping companies decided to do two things – *merge and lead*, whereas they decided to do just one thing – *merge* – and this in turn led to the formation of the world's second largest shipping company.

80. **Official Answer (OA) – D**

Concepts Tested – Comparison, Usage, Parallelism

A.   The use of *like* to give examples is incorrect. The use of *they* is ambiguous.

B.   The comparison between *colleges in America* and *developing countries* is incorrect. The use of *like* to give examples is incorrect. The use of *they* is ambiguous.

C.   The use of *they* is ambiguous.

D.   The correct answer

E.   The phrases *in America the colleges* and *Indian colleges* are not parallel.

81. **Official Answer (OA) – E**

   Concepts Tested – Parallelism, Subject Verb Agreement

   A. The singular subject *group* does not agree with the plural verb *have*.

   B. The singular subject *group* does not agree with the plural verb *have*. Since *be* comes after *not only* it needs to be repeated after *but also*

   C. The comma needs to be followed by who is trying to improve the aesthetics of the neighbourhood i.e. *the group of citizens* and not *the park*

   D. Since *be* comes before *not only*, it does not need to be repeated after *but also*

   E. The correct answer. The singular verb *has* agrees with the singular subject *group*. Also uses *be* correctly only once before *not only*.

82. **Official Answer (OA) – E**

   Concepts Tested – Usage, Pronoun Agreement

   A. The singular *a customer* does not agree with the plural pronoun *they*. Also *items* are countable, so should be modified by *fewer* and not *less*.

   B. *Items* are countable, so should be modified by fewer and not less.

   C. *Items* are countable, so should be modified by fewer and not lesser.

   D. *Items* are countable, so should be modified by fewer and not less.

   E. The correct answer.

83. **Official Answer (OA) – C**

Concepts Tested – Usage, Idiom, Parallelism

    A. The reason something happens always needs to be followed by *that*. Also another *on* is required after *than* to get the parallelism correct

    B. The reason something happens always needs to be followed by *that*. The use of the present continuous tense (*are spending*) is awkward

    C. The correct answer

    D. The present perfect tense (*have spent*) is not required because this is a general statement of truth, so needs to be in the simple present tense. Also another *on* is required after *instead of* to get the parallelism correct

    E. Wordy and awkward. Correct idiom is to *spend effort on* something

84. **Official Answer (OA) – A**

Concepts Tested – Tense

    A. The correct answer. Since Boris Becker's career is over, the correct tense has to be the simple past tense *won*

    B. The present perfect tense cannot be used for something that took place in the past, unless its effect is felt in the present which is not the case in this option.

    C. This sentence is a fragment because it doesn't have a main verb.

    D. This sentence is a fragment because it doesn't have a main verb

    E. The past perfect tense is not required since the sentence does not talk about two different past events but just one.

85. **Official Answer (OA) – C**

   Concepts Tested – Idiom, Pronoun Reference

   A. The use of *so....as to* is awkward. The use of two *being's* makes this sentence even more awkward.

   B. The use of the pronoun *he* to refer to the possessive *artist's fame* is incorrect. Also the use of *barely* and *not* together creates a double negative

   C. The correct answer, appropriately uses the idiom *so...that*

   D. This sentence is a fragment because it doesn't have a main verb.

   E. The placement of the phrase *such was his fame* next to *house* is awkward and unclear.

86. **Official Answer (OA) – E**

   Concepts Tested – Comparison, Usage

   A. Incorrectly compares *writing for magazines* with *newspaper editors*. Also *where* cannot be used to refer to *writing for magazines*.

   B. Incorrectly compares *writing for magazines* with *newspaper editors*.

   C. *Where* cannot be used to refer to *magazine editors*.

   D. Incorrectly compares *editing magazines* with *newspaper editors*.

   E. The correct answer

87. **Official Answer (OA) – C**

   Concepts Tested – Pronoun Agreement, Idiom

   A. Plural noun *employees* cannot be compared with *that*; we require *those* instead. Also the correct idiom is *forbidden to*

   B. *Contrasted to* is awkward and unidiomatic. Also the correct expression is *forbidden to discuss* and not *discussing*

   C. The use of *them* is incorrect; it should be *those* instead.

   D. The correct answer.

   E. The correct idiom is *forbidden to* and not *forbidden from*

88. **Official Answer (OA) – E**

   Concepts Tested – Comparison, Usage

   A. *Hours* is countable so needs to be modified by *fewer* and not *less*. Also the comparison of *Abraham's time* with *Andy* is incorrect; it should be with *Andy's time* instead

   B. *Cups of coffee* is countable so needs to be modified by *fewer*.

   C. Since the sentence starts with *it took*, the part after *than* should also repeat this construction. Since the *it took* is missing after *than*, this option is incorrect.

   D. The comparison of *Abraham's time* with *Andy* is incorrect; it should be with *Andy's time* instead

   E. The correct answer, correctly uses *fewer* to modify both the countable nouns – *hours and cups*. Also correctly compares the time taken by Abraham with the time taken by Andy.

89. **Official Answer (OA) – C**

   Concepts Tested – Parallelism, Meaning

   A. Uses passive clause after the comma. Since the clause before the comma (*John had prepared a comprehensive report*) is in the Active voice, the clause after the comma should also be in the Active voice.

   B. The use of *although* and *yet* in the same sentence is redundant.

   C. The correct answer

   D. The management was impressed by a contrast in John's work but this sentence does away with that contrast altogether

   E. While this sentence appears short and crisp, it suffers from the same problem as option D

90. **Official Answer (OA) – B**

   Concepts Tested – Pronoun Agreement, Idiom

   A. Since the subject is the singular *machine, their* users needs to be *its* users

   B. The correct answer. *Its* refers to *machine* and the correct idiom is *different from*.

   C. This is a trap answer. It looks better than B because it does away with the pronoun *its*. However notice that this option gets the idiom incorrect – *different than*.

   D. Since the subject is the singular *machine, their* users needs to be *its* users

   E. *However* needs to be preceded by a semi colon and not by a comma. The correct idiom is *different from*

91. **Official Answer (OA) – D**

Concepts Tested – Tense, Run on Sentence

It is tough to determine whether this sentence should be in the simple past or the past perfect tense (*was or had been*) – the past perfect tense will be correct in this case. Look at it this way – *Friday evening* definitely is a time in the past and the signing of the petition obviously started before this. So the sentence does talk about two events at different times in the past and you use the past perfect tense to refer to the earlier event i.e. *the signing.*

A. Gets the tense right but the use of *them* after the comma leads to a run-on sentence. Also the singular verb *has* does not agree with the plural *they*

B. The use of the simple past tense *was* is incorrect. The use of *them* after the comma leads to a run-on sentence. The use of *having had* is also awkward.

C. The use of the present perfect tense *have left* is incorrect since the sentence is talking about something that was the case on Friday evening (so we should use the simple past tense *left*)

D. The correct answer.

E. Same problems as B. Additionally the use of *and* is not required.

92. **Official Answer (OA) – E**

Concepts Tested – Modifiers, Tense

A. The sentence starts with a modifying phrase so whoever is doing the research needs to come after the comma i.e. *Professor Roberts.* Since the sentence is in the simple past tense the correct verb should be *ended* and not *end*

B. The use of past continuous tense (*were encouraging*) is not required. The construction of the sentence is passive and very awkward.

C. In the phrase *these systems, these* doesn't make any sense because these systems haven't been mentioned earlier. The placement of the modifying phrase at the end of the sentence is incorrect.

D. The use of *they* in the clause *they were meant to encourage* is ambiguous – we don't know whether *they* refers to the *workers* or to *modern production systems.*

E. The correct answer

93. **Official Answer (OA) – D**

Concepts Tested – Subjunctive Mood

A. The use of *recommend* should signal that we need to use the subjunctive mood in this sentence. The use of *recommend* and *should* in the same sentence is redundant.

B. In the subjunctive mood, *recommended* should be followed by *that*. Also the use of *should* is again redundant

C. In the subjunctive mood, the use of the infinitive *to vacate* is incorrect

D. The correct answer

E. The use of *recommend* and *must* together creates an oxymoron. *Must* means compulsion and *recommend* implies suggestion so the two cannot be used together

94. **Official Answer (OA) – D**

Concepts Tested – Tense

A. The restructuring agency has done two things which need to be placed in the same tense. *Explored* in the simple past tense is not consistent with *has not found* in the present perfect tense. You need to go with the simple past tense *did not find* to make this correct.

B. The past perfect tense *had explored* is not consistent with the present perfect tense *has not found*.

C. *Did not found* is an incorrect phrase – you need the base form of the verb after *did not* i.e. *find* and not *found* (which itself is in the simple past tense)

D. The correct answer; places both the actions in the present perfect tense.

E. The present perfect *has explored* is not consistent with the simple past tense *did not find*.

95. **Official Answer (OA) – D**

   Concepts Tested – Meaning, Modifiers

   A. The use of *its* is ambiguous as it could refer to *Iceland* and it could also refer to *fresh water*. Also the plural subject (because of the use of *and*) does not agree with the singular verb *makes*.

   B. The subject verb agreement is correct because of the use of the additive phrase (making the singular *supply* the subject). However the problem of *its* being ambiguous remains.

   C. The modifying phrase at the beginning of the sentence needs to come closer to *location*. Also the singular subject *supply* does not agree with the plural *make*.

   D. The correct answer. The use of *its* is not ambiguous because it comes before any other noun (such as *water*) has been mentioned. The modifying phrase is also placed close to *location*

   E. Makes it appear as though Iceland has location, which is absurd. Also doesn't make it clear that Iceland is a natural nesting location because of those two factors.

96. **Official Answer (OA) – D**

   Concepts Tested – Parallelism, Usage

   A. You can't be criticized *in* something but *for* something. Also the three things that need to be parallel are – *curb, improve, and devise*

   B. The last part after the comma is disconnected from the rest of the sentence. There is no parallel structure in the sentence

   C. Don't be fooled by *failing, improving, devising*. The three things that need to be parallel are – *curb, improve, and devise*.

   D. The correct answer

   E. *Failing* and *improving* are not parallel to *devise*

97. **Official Answer (OA) – C**

   Concepts Tested – Meaning, Parallelism

   A. Since aboard comes after *either*, a preposition needs to come after *or* as well - *on* needs to be used before station platforms. Also the connector among the four things – *smoke, drink, eat, play loud music* – needs to be *or* because the use of *and* only implies that all four of these cannot be done together.

   B. The use of *to* in *to play loud music* breaks the parallel structure. Since *aboard* comes after *either*, a preposition needs to come after *or* as well - *on* needs to be used before *station platforms*.

   C. The correct answer.

   D. To maintain parallelism, there should be a *to* before *play loud music*.

   E. Since *aboard* comes after *either*, a preposition needs to come after *or* as well - *on* needs to be used before *station platforms*

98. **Official Answer (OA) – A**

   Concepts Tested – Subject Verb Agreement

   A. The correct answer

   B. The subject is plural *shareholders*, which does not agree with the singular *has*

   C. Wordy. The use of *for implementing* is unidiomatic

   D. The subject is plural *shareholders*, which does not agree with singular *has*

   E. The subject is plural *shareholders* and the *Board of Directors*, which does not agree with singular *has*

99. **Official Answer (OA) – E**

Concepts Tested – Parallelism

A. The three items in the list – *siphoning, invented, lied* – are not parallel

B. The correct idiom to show accusation is *charged with.*

C. The correct idiom to show accusation is *charged with.*

D. The use of *for* before *inventing* and *having lied* breaks the parallelism

E. The correct answer.

100. **Official Answer (OA) – D**

Concepts Tested – Subject Verb Agreement, Pronoun Agreement

A. The singular subject *every one* requires the singular verb *has.* Also it cannot be replaced by the plural pronoun *they*

B. The singular subject *every one* requires the singular verb *has.* The use of the adverb *compulsorily* to modify the noun *search* doesn't make sense; you instead require the adjective *compulsory.*

C. The singular subject *every one* requires the singular verb *has.*

D. The correct answer

E. The singular subject *every one* cannot be replaced by the plural pronoun *they*

101. **Official Answer (OA) – C**

   Concepts Tested – Parallelism, Idiom

   A. Since *cater* comes before *not only*, it must apply to whatever comes after *but also* as well. So it doesn't make sense to put *help* after *but also* because you can't *cater and help*. *Conducting research* needs to be followed by the preposition *on*. *Conducting research* is not parallel to *conservation of*. Finally the correct idiom is *help to do* and not *help in doing*

   B. Since *cater* comes before *not only*, it must apply to whatever comes after *but also* as well. So it doesn't make sense to put *aid* after *but also* because you can't *cater and aid*. *Conducting research* needs to be followed by the preposition *on*

   C. The correct answer.

   D. Plural *zoos* does not agree with the singular *caters*. *Conducting research* needs to be followed by the preposition *on*

   E. The correct idioms are *aid in conducting* or *help to conduct*; this one incorrectly combines the two. Also *conservation of* should be preceded by the preposition *in* (*in the conservation of*)

102. **Official Answer (OA) – D**

   Concepts Tested – Pronoun reference

   A. The use of *they* is ambiguous as it could refer to *men, shirts, or jeans*.

   B. The use of *although* and *but* in the same sentence is redundant. The use of *they* is still ambiguous.

   C. The use of *they* is ambiguous as it could refer to *men, shirts, or jeans*.

   D. The correct answer; does away with the pronoun altogether.

   E. The opening modifying phrase incorrectly refers to *men*.

103. **Official Answer (OA) – D**

Concepts Tested – Subject Verb Agreement, Idiom

A. The subject *one* does not agree with the plural *are estimated*. Also the correct idiom is *estimated to be*.

B. The subject *one* does not agree with the plural *are estimated*

C. The singular *has been excavated* does not agree with the plural subject *artefacts*. The correct idiom is *estimated to be*.

D. The correct answer

E. The singular *has been excavated* does not agree with the plural subject *artefacts*.

104. **Official Answer (OA) – D**

Concepts Tested – Pronoun Agreement, Pronoun Case, Run-on sentence

A. This is a run-on sentence since *however* cannot be used to connect two independent clauses. *Who* is the wrong pronoun case, we require the objective case *whom*. The plural *they* does not agree with the singular *trust* and the singular *it* does not agree with the plural *loans*

B. This is a run-on sentence since *however* cannot be used to connect two independent clauses. The plural *they* does not agree with the singular *trust*

C. The plural *they* does not agree with the singular *trust*

D. The correct answer

E. *Who* is the wrong pronoun case, we require the objective case *whom*

105. **Official Answer (OA) – D**

   Concepts Tested – Modifiers

   A. The use of *lay* is incorrect; a person always *lies* down

   B. The use of the infinitive *to rest* makes it appear as though the woodcutter decided to do two things whereas he just decided to do one thing

   C. The use of the comma after *woodcutter* is incorrect as this is not a modifying phrase or a non essential clause. The use of *lay* is incorrect; a person always *lies* down. The use of the infinitive *to rest* makes it appear as though the woodcutter decided to do two things whereas he just decided to do one thing

   D. The correct answer

   E. There needs to be a conjunction connecting *toiled* and *decided*.

106. **Official Answer (OA) – C**

   Concepts Tested – Subject Verb Agreement, Meaning, Run-on Sentence

   A. The singular subject phrase *illegal addition* does not agree with the plural *are*. The part after the comma creates a run-on sentence. Also it is not clear whether the hotel owes money to the other two hotels or whether the other two hotels also owe money to the exchequer.

   B. The use of *and* does not make any sense. Also it is not clear whether the hotel owes money to the other two hotels or whether the other two hotels also owe money to the exchequer.

   C. The correct answer

   D. The singular subject phrase *illegal addition* does not agree with the plural *are*. The part after the comma creates a run-on sentence.

   E. The singular subject *it* (because of the use of the additive *as well as*) does not agree with the plural verb *owe*

107. **Official Answer (OA) – D**

Concepts Tested – Parallelism

A. *Learning* is not parallel with *to learn*

B. The comparison between *learning* and *playing* does not make sense; *learning* should be common to both the actions and *driving* and *playing* should actually be parallel.

C. Since the sentence talks about *acquiring* like skills, *learning* cannot be omitted from the sentence.

D. The correct answer

E. Same as B.

108. **Official Answer (OA) – E**

Concepts Tested – Tense, Parallelism

A. Since the sentence talks about a completed action in the future, you need to use the future perfect tense (*will have completed*). Another problem with this option is that it does not maintain parallelism by making the last part passive – *and more than seventy hours spent* – which doesn't have any meaning.

B. You require the future perfect tense (*will have completed*) and not the simple future tense (*will complete*). You need an *and* before *three hundred practice questions*.

C. Since we are talking about the future in the present time, the use of *would* is incorrect.

D. Same as C. The parallelism is also not maintained.

E. The correct answer. He *will have completed......and spent* also gets the parallelism right.

109. **Official Answer (OA) – C**

   Concepts Tested – Subject Verb agreement, Modifiers, Tense

   A. We require the adverb *consistently* to modify the adjective *rising*. Also the plural subject *revenues* does not agree with the singular verb *has*

   B. The plural subject *revenues* does not agree with the singular verb *has*

   C. The correct answer. Here the subject is *rise* so the use of the singular verb *has* is correct.

   D. The use of past tense *was* is incorrect since the sentence is in the present tense

   E. The singular subject *rise* does not agree with the plural verb *have*

110. **Official Answer (OA) – D**

   Concepts Tested – Usage, Tense

   A. *Where* can only be used to refer to a location, not to a subject. Use *in which* instead. Also the tenses are inconsistent. Barry studied first and scored marks later so the studying should ideally be in the past perfect tense (*had*)

   B. Same as A. The tense is correct in this one though.

   C. Same as A (there is a *where* at the end of this option, in case you didn't notice). The tense is also inconsistent.

   D. The correct answer.

   E. Incorrect use of *where* and inconsistent tenses.

111. **Official Answer (OA) – E**

   Concepts Tested – Parallelism

   A. *Battery that lasts longer* is not parallel to *faster processor* and *sleeker design*.

   B. Same as A

   C. The use of of *having* is awkward and unidiomatic. Also the phrase *more sleeker* is redundant

   D. The plural *they* cannot refer to the singular *ultrabook*

   E. The correct answer

112. **Official Answer (OA) – C**

   Concepts Tested – Idiom, Usage, Run-on Sentence

   A. *Where* cannot be used to refer to a process, use *in which* instead. Also the correct idiom is a term *refers* to something or someone

   B. This is a run-on sentence.

   C. The correct answer. Does away with the run-on by making the first clause dependent on the second by the use of *while*

   D. This is a run-on sentence. Also *when* cannot refer to a *process*.

   E. *Where* cannot be used to refer to a *process*. Also distorts the meaning by suggesting that the term has several meanings in scientific terminology

113. **Official Answer (OA) – B**

Concepts Tested – Comparison

A. The comparison is incorrect. While *that* can refer back to *performance*, you are in essence comparing the performance of the iron and steel industry this year with the performance of any other year, but with whose performance?

B. The correct answer. This gets the comparison correct. It basically states that the performance of the iron and steel industry has been better this year than (it has been) in any other year. The use of the preposition *in* makes all the difference

C. *Better* always takes *than*. Also the comparison of *performance* with *any other year* is incorrect

D. Same as C

E. That in the phrase *that of any other year's performance* has no antecedent.

114. **Official Answer (OA) – E**

Concepts Tested – Subject Verb Agreement, Meaning

A. The use of *raising* is incorrect as no one is actually raising the raw material costs; the correct modifier should be *rising*. Also the subject is raw material *costs* i.e. plural, so the use of the singular verb *has* is incorrect.

B. In this case we have a compound subject – *rising and escalating* – so the verb should be the plural *have* and not the singular *has*

C. This sentence gets the subject verb agreement correct because the subject is the singular *rise*. However notice that *the rise in raw material costs* has an action noun (*the rise*) whereas *escalating corporate tax rates* is a simple gerund phrase. The two cannot be parallel to each other.

D. Again the subject is raw material *costs* i.e. plural, so the use of the singular verb *has* is incorrect.

E. The correct answer

115. **Official Answer (OA) – C**

Concepts Tested – Modifiers, Meaning

    A. The phrase *to exist in space on a two-dimensional surface* makes it appear as if the figures are literally in some space on the surface. Also *where* cannot modify *a system*, use *in which* instead

    B. The placement of the prepositional phrase *on a two-dimensional surface* is very confusing. Also *where* cannot modify *a system*, use *in which* instead

    C. The correct answer. The figures are actually on a two dimensional surface but the artist is trying to make it look as if they are in space. The use of *in which* to modify *system* is also correct.

    D. Same as A

    E. Passive construction is awkward and wordy. The modifying phrase *a mathematical system.....* incorrectly modifies *The Renaissance Art period*. The use of *where* is incorrect.

116. **Official Answer (OA) – E**

Concepts Tested – Subject Verb Agreement, Meaning

    A. The singular subject *reduction* does not agree with the plural verbs *have* and *are*.

    B. While this sentence looks correct, there is a slight ambiguity in meaning. Ideally *that* should restrict *reduction* and not *ratios*. Also this sentence incorrectly suggests that *ratios* have taken place in the last decade.

    C. The singular subject *reduction* does not agree with the plural verb *are*

    D. Same as B. Also the singular subject *reduction* does not agree with the plural verb *have*

    E. The correct answer. Correctly uses *that* to modify *reduction*. Also uses the singular verb *is* to agree with the singular subject *reduction*.

117. **Official Answer (OA) – D**

    Concepts Tested – Parallelism, Meaning

    A. The activist has done two things that need to be made parallel – *railed against the callousness and the negligence and tried to forge something.* So there needs to be an *and* between *callousness* and *negligence*

    B. The use of the infinitive *to rail* after the comma is incorrect. Also *to rail* is not parallel *to trying*

    C. This construction tries to make three things parallel – *has spent, railed, and tried.* This is obviously incorrect as the sentence does not try to convey this. Also the *and* is missing before *negligence*

    D. The correct answer.

    E. The *and* is missing before *neglecting.* Also the use of *neglecting* changes the meaning of the sentence by suggesting that the upper classes are being neglected

118. **Official Answer (OA) – B**

    Concepts Tested – Subject Verb Agreement, Usage

    A. The singular *group* does not agree with the plural *have promised. Do so* is always preferred to *do it*

    B. The correct answer

    C. Has *continue* to work is incorrect; the verb should be *has continued and will continue.*

    D. The singular *group* does not agree with the plural *they. Do so* is always preferred to *do it*

    E. Since the *group* is still working we should use the present perfect tense (*has worked*) and not the simple past tense (*worked*). The singular *group* does not agree with the plural *have promised* and the plural *they*

119. Official Answer (OA) – C

Concepts Tested – Parallelism, Meaning

A. The question to ask is how many things has the Labour Department approved? Only two – *an increase and a reduction*. This entire action is bringing joy to the immigrant labourers. So A obviously gets the parallelism wrong by not putting an *and* between *increase* and *reduction* and by using *brought* as a verb to parallel *approved*

B. Incorrectly suggests that the wage increase has reduced the workers' tax obligations.

C. The correct answer. Uses *bringing* as an adverbial modifier to modify the action of the entire preceding clause.

D. The subjunctive mood does not have to be used with verbs such as approved. Also making *approved* and *brought* parallel makes no logical sense.

E. The use of *increase* before *both* suggests that there was an increase in the reduction of the workers tax obligation as well which is absurd. Also the use of *both* always requires *and* and not *along with*.

120. Official Answer (OA) – E

Concepts Tested – Tense, Pronoun Agreement, Usage

A. The plural *their* does not agree with the singular *team*. Also to refer to a future event always use the simple future tense (*will win*) and not the present continuous tense (*are going to win*)

B. Same as A

C. Looks correct but notice that this sentence is in the past tense (*promised*). Hence, the use of *will* is incorrect, use *would* instead.

D. The use of *would* with the present *has promised* is incorrect. The modifying phrase at the end should be closer to *the rugby team*.

E. The correct answer

121. **Official Answer (OA) – D**

   Concepts Tested – Comparison, Idiom

   A. The use of the apostrophe at the end of *players* is incorrect because *that* in the phrase *that of most other players* already refers to the other players' style of batting.

   B. The correct idiom is *different from*. Also the sentence is a fragment since it is missing the main verb

   C. Incorrectly compares *Sachin Tendulkar's style of batting* with *most other players* and not with their style of batting. Also the correct idiom is *different from*

   D. The correct answer

   E. This sentence is a fragment since it does not contain a main verb (because of the use of *that*)

122. **Official Answer (OA) – D**

   Concepts Tested – Usage

   A. The use of *due to* is incorrect in the context of this sentence. The use of *being* is awkward.

   B. The use of *due to* is incorrect in the context of this sentence. Also the sentence talks about the absence of two things so the preposition *of* should be repeated before *central authority*

   C. The part after *nor* distorts the meaning of the sentence by suggesting that the problem is that the claims cannot be verified by a central authority. However, the problem is actually the absence of such a central authority.

   D. The correct answer.

   E. Same as C.

123. **Official Answer (OA) – E**

    Concepts Tested – Usage, Meaning

    A. The phrase *addition of many additional steps* is redundant ans awkward. It's better to say *addition of many steps*.

    B. The use of *it* after *and* is not required since it is understood that the subject is the process of selection. Again the phrase *addition of many additional steps* is redundant.

    C. This sentence looks correct but the last part is actually distorting the meaning by suggesting that the amendments led to many additional steps. The amendments did not lead to the steps but to the addition of the steps to the process. So this option is incorrect.

    D. Since the modifications were in the past but their effect is still felt, we need the present perfect tense (*has been*) and not the simple present tense (*is*). The phrase *addition of many additional steps* is redundant. It's better to say *addition of many steps*.

    E. The correct answer

124. **Official Answer (OA) – C**

    Concepts Tested – Subject Verb Agreement, Pronoun Agreement

    A. The singular subject *each* does not agree with the plural pronoun *their*

    B. The singular subject *every* one does not agree with the plural pronoun *their*

    C. The correct answer with the singular pronoun *its*

    D. The plural subject *all* does not agree with the singular pronoun *its*

    E. The singular subject *every* does not agree with the plural pronoun *their*

125. **Official Answer (OA) – E**

   Concepts Tested – Parallelism

   A. Since the subject *Dave* comes after *not only*, it needs to be repeated after *but also*.

   B. *Not only* requires a *but also*

   C. Since the subject *Dave* comes after *not only*, it needs to be repeated after *but also*.

   D. Wordy. The use of *each* doesn't make sense

   E. The correct answer.

PART 5

Quick Recall

The purpose of this section is to give you all the important rules/concepts discussed in this book in one place. Go through this section before you take a full length practice test so that all the Sentence Correction rules are fresh in your mind.

General approach to SC Questions

- Do not read all the options completely
- Always read vertically and try to split up the options
- Split using first words, last words, idioms, pronouns, etc.
- Pay attention to the non underlined part of the sentence

Run-ons & Fragments

- Complete Sentence = Subject + Predicate + Meaning
- If one of the above is missing, the sentence is a fragment
- Watch out for Fragment trap with relative clauses
- Run-on Sentences use a comma to connect two independent clauses
- How to Correct Run-ons
  - Use full stop
  - Use semi colon
  - Use a FANBOYS conjunction
  - Make one clause dependent on the other
- Conjunctive adverbs – *however, thus, nonetheless, etc.* – must be preceded by a semi colon and followed by a comma
- Run on trap – use of semi colon and coordinating conjunction together

Subject Verb Agreement

- Subject is before the preposition
- When connecting two nouns using additives – *as well as, along with, together with, etc.* – the subject will be the first noun (most likely singular)
- Only *and* makes compound subjects.
  - Exception to the *and* rule – when the two things are taken as one unit
- Either or/neither nor – Get the verb to agree with the subject closer to it
- Each/Every are always singular

- *The number* is singular

- *A number* is plural

- Expressions of Quantity can be singular of plural

  - *Half the money is stolen*

  - *Half the books are stolen*

- *One of the plural noun + that/who* constructions will always take a plural verb

- Some indefinite pronouns – *some, any, none, most, all* - can be singular or plural.

Tenses

- Will test you on time periods

- Don't get too technical; try to understand the meaning of the sentence

- Pay extra attention to the part that is not underlined

- Simple and Perfect tenses are important

- Prefer simple tenses to perfect tenses

- Avoid the continuous tense – *ing* – as much as possible

- Use past perfect tense – had + past participle – only when a sentence talks about two past events that took place at different times.

- The past perfect will refer to the earlier of the two events and the simple past tense to the latter one

- Do not use the present continuous tense to refer to future events. Use the simple future tense instead

- If…..Then constructions

  - If you exercise, you will become healthy

  - If you exercised, you would become healthy

  - If you had exercised, you would have become healthy

Pronouns

- Pronoun reference – a pronoun should ideally refer to one noun

  - Avoid pronouns as much as possible

  - Possessive pronouns can only refer to possessive nouns

- Pronoun Agreement

  - Be careful between *that* (singular) and those (plural)

- Pronoun Case
  - Subject Case – *I, he, she, they, etc.*
  - Object Case – *Me, her, him, them, etc.*
  - Possessive Case – *My, mine, his, her's, their's, etc.*
  - In compound structures (Debbi and I), drop the other noun to make out which pronoun to go with
- *That* is restrictive and *which* is non restrictive
- The Rule for *Which*
  - Must come after a comma
  - Must refer to the noun immediately before the comma
  - Exception – When *which* comes after a preposition such as *in which, of which, etc.*
- *Who* (subject case) and *Whom* (object case)
  - If the answer is *him* the question is *Whom*
  - If the answer is *he* the question is *who*
- Always prefer *do so* to *do it*
- Do not shift between *one* and *you*

Modifiers

- Adjectives modify nouns or pronouns
- Adverbs modify verbs, adjectives, and even other adverbs
- Be careful of choices between adjectives and adverbs – *regular/regularly, economical/economically, etc.*
- A modifier must be as close as possible to the subject it is modifying
- Adjectival Phrases/ Noun modifiers
  - modify nouns and pronouns
  - must touch the noun or pronoun it modifies
- Adverbial Phrases
  - modify the entire action of the preceding clause
  - don't have to follow the Touch rule
- Misplaced Modifier
  - Put the subject immediately next to the modifying phrase

- o Modifying phrase will mostly start with an *ing* word

    - o Running very quickly, the race was won by Usain Bolt (Incorrect)

    - o Running very quickly, Usain Bolt won the race (Correct)

- Dangling Modifier

    - o The sentence doesn't contain a subject, so add one

    - o Using a stethoscope, heartbeats can be detected (Incorrect)

    - o Using a stethoscope, a doctor can detect heartbeats (Correct)

- The Possessive trap

    - o Coming out of the office, John's laptop was stolen (Incorrect)

    - o Coming out of the office, John was robbed of his laptop (Correct)

- The use of back-to-back modifying phrases is always incorrect

Parallelism

- Correlative Conjunctions

    - o Include word pairs that are always used together such as *either …..or, not only….but also,* etc.

    - o The construction after the first word has to be repeated after the second word

- Pay attention to the meaning of the sentence to figure out what aspects to make parallel

- Simple Gerund Phrases cannot be parallel to Complex Gerund Phrases or Action nouns

- Complex Gerund Phrases can be parallel to Action Nouns

- Present participle can be parallel to a Past participle

- Sometimes it may be necessary to use *that* twice in a sentence

- Commonly used Parallelism Markers

    - o *And*

    - o *Or*

    - o *Either…..or*

    - o *Neither….nor*

    - o *Not only/just…..but also*

    - o *Both…….and*

Comparison

- Compare apples with apples and oranges with oranges
- Be careful of the comparative and superlative forms
- *More/less* always takes a *than* and not *in comparison/as compared to*
- *As many as/as much as* always takes another *as* and not *than*
- *Like* and *As*
    - Use *Like* to compare nouns
    - Use *As* to compare everything else
    - If confused go with *as*
    - Never use *like* to give examples, use *such as* instead

Meaning

- Chose from two grammatically correct options
- Always read the part that is not underlined
- Ways of distorting the Meaning
    - Ambiguous placement of Modifiers
        - *They noticed a cup on the table made of glass*
    - Incorrect use of Conjunctions
        - *John is a good student so he did poorly on the test*
    - Ambiguous Pronoun reference
        - *Joe and Paul went shopping and he fell down*
    - Faulty Comparison
        - *The flowers in my garden are more beautiful than your car*
    - Incorrect Parallelism
        - *The benefits to the company included increase in sales, productivity, and employee attrition rate.*

Idioms, Style, and Usage

- Go through the idiom list on page 132 of this book
- Avoid wordiness as much as possible
  - o Watch out for redundant phrases
- Avoid *Being*
- Avoid *ing* constructions
- Avoid the Passive voice
- Subjunctive Mood
  - o Hypothetical situations (if, wish, etc.)
    - ▪ Always use *were* and *would*
    - ▪ If I were rich I would buy a BMW
  - o Verbs such as *insist, suggest, recommend, demand*, etc
    - ▪ Must be followed by *that* and the infinitive form of the verb without the *to*
    - ▪ I recommend that the proposal be passed
- *Where* can only refer to a place. For other cases use 'in which'
  - o The town where I was born is known for its fishermen (Correct)
  - o The company where I work has gone bankrupt (Incorrect)
  - o The company in which I work has gone bankrupt (Correct)
- *Whether* and *If*
  - o Use *If* to make a conditional statement
    - ▪ If it rains, I will carry an umbrella
  - o Use *Whether* to evaluate alternatives
    - ▪ I can't decide whether I should have a pizza or a burger
  - o Never use *If* to evaluate alternatives
  - o If confused go with *whether*
- *For* and *Since*
  - o Use *For* to convey duration
    - ▪ I have been waiting for the past two hours
  - o Use *Since* to convey when a particular action started
    - ▪ I have been waiting since 2'o clock
  - o *For* can be used with any tense
  - o *Since* cannot be used with the past tense

- *Like* and *Such as*
    - Use *like* to compare nouns
    - Use *such as* to give examples (never use *like*)
- Use *only* as an adjective and not as an adverb
- *Due to* and *Because of*
    - Use *due to* only to replace *caused by*
    - If confused go with *because of*
- *Less* and *Fewer*
    - Use less to modify uncountable nouns
    - Use fewer to modify countable nouns
- *Greater* and *More*
    - Use greater….than to compare uncountable nouns
    - Use more…than to compare countable nouns
- Will, Would, and Should
    - Use *will* to refer to future in the present
    - Use *would* to refer to future in the past
    - Use *should* to make a suggestion
    - Use of *should* along with *recommend, suggest, etc.* is redundant
- *Between* and *Among*
    - Use *between* for two things and *among* for more than two things
- The possessive form of plural words only takes the apostrophe sign (') without the *s* at the end
- The use of comma
    - To set off modifying phrases
- Whenever the sentence contains words such as *barely, scarcely, hardly, etc.* always check for double negatives
    - I had barely not completed the test when the bell rang (Incorrect)
    - I had barely completed the test when the bell rang. (Correct

Concluding Notes:

Through this book we have endeavoured to provide you with all the Sentence Correction rules and concepts tested on the GMAT in one place. This book has been written in a lucid, easy to understand style; in fact we have made a conscious effort to avoid grammar jargon as much as possible and focus on understanding the meaning of sentences instead.

While we have tried to ensure that the book is completely free of errors, in case you do spot one please post it on the SC Grail 3rd edition thread on the Forums section of our website. Also in case there are some concepts that you could not understand from the book or that you would like to discuss with us, please post the same on our forums and we'll respond to you within 48 hours.

We also welcome any other feedback that you may have on how we can make the next edition of this book even better; do mail us the same on feedback@aristotleprep.com

We wish you all the best for your preparation.

The SC Grail 3rd ed Editorial Team

If you found this book useful, do check out the other book in our Grail series:

The CR Grail

Here are some standout features of the CR Grail:

- In depth coverage of all CR Question Types tested on the GMAT

- Dedicated chapter for 'Provide a Logical Conclusion' Questions – a new question type increasingly tested on the GMAT

- Brand new 100 question practice set for Intensive practice

- Jargon free and diagram free language with focus on understanding the meaning of arguments

- Quick Recall chapter at the end that provides a quick revision of all CR concepts discussed in the book

Made in the USA
Las Vegas, NV
15 January 2022